RIFLES & COMBAT SHOTGUNS

ASSAULT & SNIPER RIFLES

Brassey's Modern Military Equipment
Series Editor: James Marchington

Current Titles:

Tanks: Main Battle and Light Tanks
Marsh Gelbart

Anti-Tank Weapons
John Norris

Handguns and Sub-Machine Guns
James Marchington

Knives: Military Edged Tools & Weapons
James Marchington

NBC: Nuclear, Biological and Chemical Warfare on the Modern Battlefield
John Norris and Will Fowler

Brassey's *Modern Military Equipment*

RIFLES & COMBAT SHOTGUNS

ASSAULT & SNIPER RIFLES

John Norris

First English Edition 1997

UK editorial offices: Brassey's, 33 John Street, London WC1N 2AT
UK orders: Marston Book Services, PO Box 269, Abingdon, OX14 4SD

North American orders: Brassey's Inc., PO Box 960,
Herndon, VA 22070, USA

John Norris has asserted his moral right to be identified
as the author of this work.

Library of Congress Cataloging-in-Publication Data

Norris, John A.
Rifles and combat shotguns: assault and sniper rifles / John A. Norris
p. cm. – (Brassey's modern military equipment series)
Includes bibliographical references.
ISBN 1-85753-214-7
1. Rifles. 2. Shotguns. I. Title. II. Series: Brassey's modern military equipment.
UD390.N67 1997
623.4'425–dc21
97-33241 CIP

British Library Cataloguing in Publication Data
A catalogue record for this book is available from the British Library

ISBN 1 85753 214 7 Hardcover

Typeset & Designed by Harold Martin & Redman Ltd
Printed in Great Britain by the University Press, Cambridge.

CONTENTS

ACKNOWLEDGEMENTS

I would like to extend my sincere thanks to all the manufacturers and individuals who helped to make this work possible by supplying photographs, information and encouragement.

ACR: Advanced Combat Rifle.

AK: Avtomat Kalashnikova (Russian).

AK: Automatische Karabiner (Swiss).

AKM: Avtomat Kalashnikova Modernizirovannyi.

AKS: Avtomat Kalashnikova Skladyvayushchimsaya.

Ammunition: Unit fired by a rifle, comprising a cartridge case containing propellant, projectile (bullet) and primer cap.

AP: Armour piercing. Some small arms ammunition is of the armour piercing type to allow the engagement of light armoured vehicles.

Aperture sight: Type of sight that uses a small hole aperture as the rear element.

ASARS: Army Small Arms Requirements Studies.

AUG: Armee Universal Gewehr.

Ball: Standard rifle ammunition with a single projectile.

Ballistics: The science of understanding and measuring the performance of the propellant, primer and projectile.

Ballistite: Propellant used in blank cartridge which may be used to launch a rifle grenade from the muzzle of a rifle.

Barleycorn (sight): Front sight in shape of grain of corn or wheat.

Barrel: Tubular part of rifle through which the projectile is fired and given direction.

Barrel band: Band used to attach the rifle's barrel to the fore-end of the weapon.

Bent: A notch cut in the weapon's bolt, striker or hammer into which the sear engages to hold component in readiness to fire.

BFA: Blank Firing Attachment. A device secured to the muzzle of a rifle's barrel and intended to restrict the emission of gases from the barrel when firing blank rounds. The BFA is used for training purposes.

Blank: Type of small arms ammunition which does not contain a projectile. It is identical in size to a round of 'ball' ammunition, but contains only propellant powder. When fired from a weapon fitted with a BFA (qv) it simulates actual firing of the weapon.

Bolt: Moving part of a rifle which closes against the breech end of the barrel to load a round and hold it in place as it is fired.

Bolt action: Type of rifle in which the breech bolt is operated by hand – most commonly found on sporting and sniping rifles.

Bore: The hole down the length of the barrel along which the bullet is propelled. The term 'bore' can also describe the internal diameter of the barrel, as in '12-bore shotgun'.

Bottle necked: A cartridge case in which the diameter is reduced at the opening to accommodate the bullet, which has a smaller diameter than the body of the case.

Box magazine: A fixed or detachable metal box which holds ammunition ready to be fed into the breech.

Breech: The rear end of a barrel into which ammunition is loaded.

Bullet: A projectile fired from a rifle.

Bullpup: A rifle in which the mechanism is laid out to reduce the overall length of the weapon. The magazine is generally located behind the pistol grip and the receiver is set against the firer's shoulder.

Butt: Part of the rifle held against the firer's shoulder.

CAL: Carabine Automatique Légère.

Calibre: Diameter of weapon's bore measured across the rifling lands.

Cap: Primer assembly at the rear of a cartridge case, which is struck by the firing pin to fire the round.

Carbine: Term used to denote a short rifle. No longer in military usage.

Cartridge: A round of ammunition comprising case, cap, propellant and projectile.

Cartridge case: Brass shell containing propellant and primer cap.

Cartridge headspace: The distance between the face of the bolt or breech-block and the base of the cartridge case when the weapon is loaded.

Caseless: A cartridge which has no metal casing. The propellant is formed into a solid block which also serves to support the bullet and primer cap.

Centre fire: Cartridge case which has the primer cap located centrally at its base.

Chamber: Part of the barrel into which the cartridge is **vii** loaded ready for firing.

Choke: Constriction in shotgun barrel causing shot to disperse less than would otherwise be the case after leaving the bore.

Cook-off: Premature ignition of round due to high barrel temperature.

Cordite: Propellant used in rifle cartridges.

Cycle of operation: Process of semi-automatic rifles whereby round of ammunition is fed, chambered, fired and empty case ejected and weapon re-cocked ready for firing.

Cyclic rate of fire: Theoretical rate of fire if weapon could be fired continuously without the need to replenish magazine.

Cylinder: Shotgun barrel of same internal diameter along its whole length, with no choke – suitable for firing solid projectiles.

Ejector: Component which throws empty cartridge case away from weapon after firing.

Elevation: The angle in the vertical plane between line of sight and the bullet's trajectory.

Extractor: Component which pulls empty cartridge case from chamber after firing.

FAL: Fusil Automatique Léger.

FAMAS: Fusil Automatique de Manufacture d'Armes de St Etienne.

Feed: Portion of firing cycle during which new cartridge is removed from magazine and loaded into the chamber.

Firing pin: Component which transfers the blow of the hammer to the cartridge primer, to initiate firing.

Flash eliminator: Device fitted to muzzle of a rifle's barrel to prevent or reduce the forming of flash or flame during firing.

Flechette: Long, narrow, fin-stabilised, dart-like projectile.

Fore-end: The front part of the stock, located under the barrel, which may be held by the firer to support the weapon. Also called the forestock.

Foresight: Front element of a sighting system.

FWE: Foreign Weapons Evaluation.

Gas cylinder: Housing for the gas piston on gas operated rifles.

Gas system: System of operation of a rifle which uses propellant gases tapped from the barrel to operate the action.

Gauge: A system of bore measurement used for shotguns.

Hammer: A device held under tension by a spring until released by the trigger, which strikes the firing pin to actuate the primer of a cartridge.

Hangfire: Failure of ammunition to fire even though primer has been struck.

IRUS: Infantry Rifle Unit Study.

Lands: Raised portions of bore between rifling grooves.

Magazine follower: Plate in magazine which is pushed up by the magazine spring, on which rest the cartridges.

Magazine spring: The spring which forces the follower against the cartridges.

Mainspring: The primary spring of a trigger mechanism.

Matched ammunition: Ammunition manufactured to exceptionally close tolerances for extreme accuracy.

Misfire: Failure of a weapon or round of ammunition to fire despite being operated correctly.

MIWS: Multi-purpose Individual Weapon System.

MRTF: Mean Rounds To Failure.

Muzzle: The end of the barrel from which the projectile exits.

OEG: Occluded Eye Gunsight.

Open sights: Simple sighting system comprising rearsight and foresight elements which are aligned with the target.

Optical sight: Sighting system which makes use of optical lenses to form an image of the target, often magnified, on which an aiming mark is superimposed.

Pistol grip: The handle by the trigger mechanism by which the rifle is supported by the firing hand.

Pitch: The degree of twist in the rifling of a barrel.

Primer: Container for the detonating compound to ignite the propellant.

Propellant: Nitro-cellulose based compound which burns to provide the energy to propel the projectile from the barrel.

Pump-action: Hand-operated mechanism used in some repeating shotguns, where the fore-end is moved back to eject a spent round, and forward again to chamber the next round from the magazine.

RAW: Rifleman's Assault Weapon.

Rifling: Spiral grooves cut into the interior of barrel to impart stabilising spin to bullet.

Rimless: Cartridge with no protruding rim at its base.

Round: Complete item of ammunition, comprising bullet, cartridge case, propellant and primer.

RPM: Rounds Per Minute.

Safety: Mechanical device to prevent firing of a weapon.

SAR: Singapore Assault Rifle.

SAWES: Small Arms Weapons Effects Simulator.

Sear: Part of the firing mechanism, linked to the trigger, which engages with the hammer, firing pin or striker, and when pulled clear by trigger action allows the weapon to fire.

Selective fire: A weapon which can be made to fire either semi- or fully automatic.

Selector: Means by which a weapon can be made to fire either single rounds or fully automatic.

Shot: Pellets fired from the cartridge of a shotgun.

Sight: Device attached to a weapon to allow precise aiming.

SLR: Self-Loading Rifle.

Solid slug: Single projectile fired from a shotgun, usually with angled ridges designed to impart spin for stability in flight.

Stgw: Sturmgewehr (Swiss).

Stock: Part of a weapon shaped to fit in the firer's shoulder – often made of wood or, more recently, plastics.

StuG: Sturmgewehr (German).

Trajectory: Curved path followed by a projectile after it leaves the muzzle.

Trigger: A lever by which the firing mechanism is actuated.

Trigger guard: A protective guard fitted around the trigger to protect against accidental firing.

Trigger stop: Means of arresting travel of trigger after firing.

Twist: The spiral of the rifling within the barrel.

Velocity: Speed of a bullet's travel, usually measured close to the muzzle.

Vertex: Highest point of a bullet's trajectory.

Windage: Horizontal deviation between line of sight and the bullet's trajectory.

Yaw: Horizontal angle between a bullet's axis and its trajectory.

Zero: To adjust a rifle's sight so that the aiming point coincides with the point of impact at a given distance.

This work covers three types of weapon used by infantrymen the world over. First is the standard semi-automatic rifle, which of late has come to be termed as an assault rifle. The rifle has been the infantryman's standard weapon on the battlefield, ever since industrialisation allowed the widespread introduction of firearms. The second type of firearm covered in this work is the highly specialised and inherently accurate sniping rifle. The accuracy of this weapon, like any other, depends largely on the skill of the user, but with a good sniping rifle and 'matched' ammunition, a well trained sniper can engage targets at extreme ranges.

The third category of weapon covered in this book is the highly controversial shotgun. Some people claim the shotgun has no place in military use, but others – including many who have used it in combat – swear by it. The shotgun may not be the most accurate weapon, but at close-range it is a powerful force multiplier.

THE ASSAULT RIFLE

Over the past twenty years or so, the basic rifle of the infantryman has been the subject of many trials and experimental modifications. However, all the plans to improve the overall performance of the rifle, and make it lighter in weight, have largely come to nought. With two or three exceptions, the current range of rifles in service around the world remains basically unaltered.

One of the great non-starters was the proposed German G11 rifle, firing a 4.7mm calibre caseless round. This weapon was developed to advanced trials phase, and the prospects for its future looked good – even if the calibre was somewhat on the reduced side. The developing company had managed to overcome many design difficulties, such as 'cook-off', and the feeding and chambering of the rounds. With the end of the Cold War in 1990, the G11 programme was one of the early casualties, as both Eastern and Western powers suspended weapons development programmes. The G11 rifle never entered service.

During the 1970s a number of countries, including some NATO member states, began to conduct trials into improving conventional small arms ammunition. They also looked into the feasibility of developing specialised ammunition, including flechette rounds to penetrate body armour. But apart from re-standardising the NATO round from 7.62mm down to 5.56mm, nothing much came of these trials.

At around the same time, word began to circulate of a new design of rifle, which was to be a great departure from the standard weapon layout. What started out as rumour turned into reality when the first of the modern 'bullpup' designs entered service. In the bullpup design, the magazine is located behind the pistol grip, making the rifle considerably shorter and more easily handled, especially in confined spaces such as the interior of an armoured vehicle. The bullpup idea was not new and in fact made one of its earliest appearances on the German Model SS41 anti-tank rifle in 7.92mm calibre during the Second World War. What was new, however, was the idea of applying this design to the standard infantryman's rifle.

A flood of bullpup designs was expected in the wake of the successful introduction of the FAMAS and SA80, both in 5.56mm calibre, into the French and British

The Fusil Automatique Léger from Fabrique Nationale of Belgium. This has appeared in many versions, including a heavy barrelled model with a bipod. The Argentine Army was equipped with this rifle during the Falkland Islands War of 1982. The British Forces carried a version of this, the L1A1 self-loading rifle. Despite similarities the parts of the two designs are not compatible, but British troops found it invaluable that both weapons fired the same calibre ammunition.

Armies respectively. Several designs were proposed including the Finnish Valmet M-76 (Model 255 470), the Brazilian Model 03 LAPA/FA, and the Taiwanese Type 68, but all were dropped for one reason or another. A bullpup version of the AR18 rifle was mooted, but again nothing materialised.

At the time of writing, only three bullpup rifles are in current service: the French FAMAS, the British SA80 and the Austrian AUG. The last of these is widely considered to be the finest of the bullpup designs, and has been adopted more widely by armies around the world.

Ammunition for rifles has also undergone a change, but generally nothing more dramatic than a reduction in calibre from 7.62mm to 5.56mm. This choice of calibres was fomented by NATO and is now in almost universal use. Even Russia now favours a reduced calibre in the form of 5.45mm x 39mm as fired from the AK74 and AKS74. However, they still have a place for their 7.62mm x 39mm which is fired by the instantly recognisable AK47.

There is little evidence to suggest that any great change in assault rifles and ammunition is likely in the forseeable future. Soldiers do not readily accept changes in place of tried and tested methods. Apart from the three bullpup designs mentioned, all the assault rifles in service today are laid out in straight lines, and of the gas operated semi-automatic type. The brief flirtation with caseless ammunition has been consigned to the back of the filing cabinet. Likewise, the experiment to introduce flechettes into rifle ammunition is nowadays viewed as another historical curiosity. The infantryman feels comfortable using a rifle which is reliable and fires conventional ammunition with known properties, and is reluctant to place his trust in some new-fangled idea. After all, the difference between success and failure of a firearm on the battlefield means life or death to the infantryman.

SNIPING RIFLES

Despite the trend in reduced calibres for assault rifles, the preferred calibre for sniping rifles remains 7.62mm. There are a handful of specialised sniping rifles in 5.56mm calibre, and even some firing rounds as small as .22 inch. However, these reduced calibres are in the

Scots Guards on patrol in Hong Kong in 1971. They are carrying the L1A1 self-loading rifle, which has since been replaced in service by the L85A1.

minority, with the majority of sniping rifles using 7.62mm calibres. Similarly, the old-fashioned bolt-action system still prevails for the most part on sniping rifles, but the Israeli Galil, Russian Dragunov and Swiss SG510-4 SIG rifles are of semi-automatic designs.

There are two schools of thought governing the use of semi-automatic weapons for the purposes of sniping. One believes in the reliable bolt-action sniping rifles laid out in traditional lines and used for engaging selected targets at the optimum moment. These are seen as the 'Rolls-Royce' in sniping weaponry. The other school of thought suggests that a sniper needs a semi-automatic to protect himself should his position of concealment be compromised. There is no doubt, however, that the bolt-action is the most reliable and proven design for sniping, and is favoured by Britain's armed forces.

A sniper does more than just engage human targets. With modern armies relying heavily on sophisticated communications and surveillance equipment, a sniper can cause enormous disruption to enemy forces with a few well placed rounds. A single armour piercing round can disable an aircraft parked on a runway, or destroy a

1st Battalion Scots Guards leaving Singapore in 1965. They are all carrying the L1A1 SLR which fired the 7.62mm round.

communications satellite dish, for instance.

In recent years there has been an increase in battlefield use of heavy .50 calibre (12.7mm) sniping rifles, sometimes described as 'anti-matériel rifles'. These are generally used to target enemy equipment and installations rather than in the anti-personnel role, and as such fall outside the scope of this book.

ASSAULT SHOTGUNS

Shotguns have been used on and off by the military for some considerable time. In his definitive work on the subject, 'The World's Fighting Shotguns', Thomas F. Swearengen recounts the origins of this devastating weapon and its appeal to the military. The book details how lawmen of the American West, including the legendary figure of 'Doc' Holliday, often used a shotgun. The shotgun was also used during the American Civil War of 1861–65, and there are accounts of how some Confederate cavalrymen carried 'sawn off' or 'cut back' double-barrelled versions in saddle holsters. Shotguns were used by US troops during the Indian wars and again during the First and Second World Wars.

This weapon has undergone a transformation from

the days of the double-barrel, and single-barrel pump-action with tubular magazine. The pump-action is still in widespread use, and favoured by some for its simplicity and robust design. However, counter-terrorist agencies and specialised military units now use semi-automatic shotguns such as the Italian SPAS 12 and SPAS 15 – the latter model fed by a box magazine to make reloading easier and quicker. South Africa has developed the Protecta 12-round revolver action shotgun, which can fire a wide range of ammunition types, including non-lethal rubber balls for anti-riot use.

Ammunition for shotguns has also come a long way from the days of scattering a handful of lead pellets in a wide arc. Ammunition available for shotguns today includes rifled slugs for accuracy, special CS anti-riot gas rounds, High Explosive Anti-Tank (HEAT), flechette and illuminating cartridges. The French have developed the multi-purpose pump shotgun APAE Type, which can fire ordinary shotgun cartridges but has an interchangeable barrel to permit the user to fire anti-riot grenades using special blank cartridges. This weapon is of the standard 12 gauge, pump-action type, 1004mm in length and weighs 2.8kg. It is particularly useful to law enforcement agencies, military and paramilitary forces. Firing either buck-shot or solid rifled slug, the APAE shotgun can be used to engage targets at ranges up to 150 metres.

SERVICE HISTORY AND MANUFACTURE

Some of the weapons contained in this work may appear familiar, while others appear more as curiosities. A few only reached the prototype stage, and never entered service, but their influence on weapons design is such that it was felt that they should be included. Other weapons contained in this work may also be thought of as outdated, but their reliability is such that they are kept in service and keep turning up – perhaps in the hands of terrorist or guerrilla organisations. Some of the older weapons were manufactured in such numbers that they will remain in use somewhere in the world for many years to come.

Readers will note that some weapons developed in one country are nowadays being manufactured somewhere entirely different. This is not unusual as countries will often grant 'friendly' nations a licence to manufacture specific weapons. Such is the diversity of an infantryman's personal weaponry that keeping track of what is in use with which army is a complicated task. For example, the Israelis use M16 rifles alongside their Galil, and the British Army also uses the M16 despite the fact that the SA80 is their standard infantry rifle. Other armies are known to have a mixture of weaponry supplied from Western states, which use a NATO standard round, and the former Soviet Union, which fire calibres associated with the late Warsaw Pact. This can lead to a logistical nightmare, but that is another story.

Scots Guardsman on jungle patrol in Malaya in 1983, carrying the L1A1 SLR.

ASSAULT RIFLES

The rifle is the infantryman's personal weapon, his own tool for use on the battlefield. At the beginning of gunpowder age warfare, crude hand-held weapons were wielded by specially trained infantrymen. By the time industrialisation allowed mass-produced firearms to be made available to large numbers of infantrymen, the character of the battlefield had already altered beyond all recognition – and was still changing at a remarkable pace.

Looking at firearm developments of the nineteenth century, one can see at a glance how rapidly changes were occurring. For example, in 1838 the British Army adopted the percussion system and only two years later the Prussian Army began to re-equip with the Dreyse breech-loading 'needle gun'. By 1851 the British Army had adopted the Minie rifle and in 1866 the French Army was taking the Chassepot rifle into service. In 1884 the German Army was introducing the Mauser bolt-action rifle into service and at the same time smokeless propellants were being developed, such as the French 'Poudre B' and the British 'Cordite' in 1890, only two years after the introduction of the Lee-Metford rifle which went on to be developed into the legendary .303 inch calibre Lee-Enfield bolt-action rifle which served for many years.

The lineage charting the development of the modern assault rifle can actually be traced directly back to events in the Second World War. Studies conducted by tacticians in Germany during the inter-war years revealed that infantrymen rarely identified targets at ranges of more than 400m, while basic weapon training meant that they had only a better-than-average chance of hitting a target of 300m range. Therefore, they concluded, why produce a round which was designed to carry out to ranges in excess of 1000m? With Adolf Hitler in power and Germany undergoing rearmament the study group attempted to 'sell' their theories to the Ordnance Supply Office. Unfortunately their idea of a short 7mm round came at a time when the German Army had billions of 7.92mm rounds of ammunition. Furthermore, it is understood that Hitler was deliberating over future infantry weapon designs.

Some sources claim that Hitler did not accept the concept of new rifle designs and was actively encouraging new sub-machine gun designs to augment the MP38 and MP40 designs. Other sources claim that he was seeking weapons with increased hitting distance. Whatever the reason, the weapon firing the new 'Short' 7.92mm round was brought in by back-door methods, obviously in an effort to circumvent political bickering, and was termed the MP43. Once sold on the idea, it was Hitler himself who coined the term 'Sturmgewehr' or assault rifle. By the end of the Second World War most armies had at least one semi-automatic rifle in service, with the most notable exceptions being Britain and Japan.

With many countries all but bankrupted by the effects of the war, funding for the development of small arms was severely limited. By the time of the Korean War most armies involved in the conflict were using rifles from the period of the Second World War. In the late 1940s Britain did flirt briefly with developing a semi-automatic rifle in the form of the EM2. This was a 'bullpup' design firing a cartridge of .280 calibre. At the time America was advocating the 7.62mm round as the way to go and so the programme to develop the EM2 was cancelled. By the early 1950s America was developing the Armalite Rifle Model AR-10 and the M14 rifle, both in the newly-accepted calibre of 7.62mm. In the event, the AR-10 was shelved in favour of the M14 rifle, which had a cyclic rate of 750 rounds per minute. This rifle served the US Army well into the 1960s, and gave sterling results during the Vietnam War.

The Belgian company of Fabrique Nationale in Herstal was the only European firearms manufacturer of note to make real advances in the design and development of semi-automatic rifles, and produced the FAL in the early 1950s. One of these early models was produced for trials by Britain in 1952/53, and from this arose the L1A1 Self-Loading Rifle, or SLR, which was only replaced in the 1980s, by the SA80 rifle, following some thirty years of service.

The new standard NATO round of 7.62mm was not readily accepted in all NATO countries, with France staying with 7.5mm as used in the MAS Modèle 49. Questions regarding the power of the new round were also raised following an incident in British Guiana (subsequently known as Guyana) in 1962. A detachment of 1st Battalion Coldstream Guards was deployed to disperse a rioting crowd which had ignored requests to clear the area. As an incentive to force the crowd to break up, a single shot was ordered to be fired at the crowd. At the time, this action was considered to be minimum force, but the single 7.62mm round fired from the SLR killed three people and wounded a fourth. If ever proof as to the efficacy of a high velocity round was needed, this was it. The FN FAL was adopted in various forms by a number of other countries, including Australia and Canada who knew it as the L2A1 and C1 respectively.

The continued involvement of US forces in the Vietnam War spurred on the American company of Colt to produce in large numbers the AR-15 rifle, more commonly known as the M16. This rifle fired a 5.56mm x 45 round and, like the FN FAL, has been taken into service in various forms by many armies around the world, including limited service with the British Army. In fact the 5.56mm (.223) round is now the standard NATO round, even being used by the French Army in their FAMAS.

At about the same time the Russians were developing the ubiquitous AK47, which by the late 1970s had exceeded a production run of over 35 million weapons. The design of this rifle was influenced by the wartime German MP43. It too fires a 7.62mm round, but of 39mm length as opposed to the NATO 7.62mm round which has a length of 51mm. The basic design of the AK47 has spawned a whole range of copies, such as the Chinese Model 56. During the Cold War the infantry of armies making up the Warsaw Pact were equipped with the AK47 rifle, and it is still built under licence in some former Warsaw Pact states. Variations on the original AK47 design included the Romanian version which has a forward pistol grip fitted, and versions with folding buttstocks. The Russian equivalent of NATO's now standard 5.56mm round is the 5.45mm for use with the AK74, which was first observed in 1979. Outwardly the AK74 is virtually identical to the AK47, with few modifications other than the change of calibre.

The most dramatic development to affect the design of assault rifles has been the rise of the 'bullpup' design. Even this has not resulted in a revolution in weapon design, with the SA80, FAMAS and AUG the only bullpup designs to have been produced in any significant numbers. The Austrian-designed AUG is the most versatile of all bullpup designs and is currently in widespread service, including the Army of the Republic of Ireland, Australia and New Zealand. The French FAMAS remains in sole use with the French Armed Forces and the British Army's SA80, really the resurrected EM2, has still not been sold overseas.

For the foreseeable future, it seems likely that the assault rifle will remain a box magazine-fed weapon of conventional layout. Experiments with new weapon designs and layouts are conducted from time to time, but by and large an army will stay with what it knows and trusts. For example, the Swiss are equipped with SIG-built weapons, the Americans have the M16 from Colt and Russia has its AK47 and AK74 designs from former state arsenals.

Most assault rifles are capable of firing rifle grenades, for anti-personnel, smoke and illuminating purposes. A large number of rifles can also be fitted with 40mm grenade-launcher systems under their barrels. These include the M16 with the M203 grenade launcher and the Austrian AUG. These grenades, fired from a separate barrel, act as a force multiplier to the infantryman and permit him to fire his rifle without being inhibited by a rifle grenade fitted to the end of the barrel.

This particular rifle from the Austrian company of Steyr is called a 'universal' gun, a claim borne out by the fact that it can be configured to a variety of roles and calibres, including 9mm and 5.56mm, and fitted with different barrels to suit the conversion. There is even a heavy-barrelled version equipped with a bipod which allows it to be used in the light support weapon role.

The weapon has a delicate appearance, but this is belied by the fact that it has been adopted by a large number of armies, including the Austrian Army and the Army of the Republic of Ireland. It can be used in all extremes of climates and terrains from desert to sub-zero conditions. The design of the AUG makes extensive use of plastic components more effectively than any other rifle of its type. In short, the AUG is the most successful bullpup design rifle in use anywhere in the world.

It can be field stripped without tools down into six main components: the barrel, receiver, trigger, bolt, magazine and stock. The basic 5.56mm version of the AUG can be converted into another configuration, such as the 9mm version or short-barrelled carbine version, by simply removing the receiver and barrel and replacing

them with the appropriate type. The AUG can also be converted into a sniping rifle, which features a low telescope mount instead of the usual optical sight with integral telescope. This allows the firer to mount a specialised sniping telescope or night-vision units.

The optical sight, which is fitted as standard to the assault rifle version of the AUG, has been optimised for battle ranges, with a black reticle ring in the centre of the field of vision. This allows the firer to place the sight onto a man-sized target and engage it at 300m ranges.

There are several aspects of this rifle which make it instantly recognisable: the high set optical sight in its standard form, the large buttstock, a forward hand grip which can be folded, and the distinctive handguard which forms part of the pistol grip. The magazine well is located behind the pistol grip in the traditional bullpup layout. The weapon can be quickly and easily converted to suit either left-handed or right-handed firers. This is done simply by changing the ejector from one side of the bolt to the other, and rotating the ejection port over to the

Troops of the Austrian Army carrying the Steyr AUG rifle in sub-zero mountain warfare conditions.

preferred side.

The receiver unit of the AUG is manufactured from aluminium die-casting which includes the seating for the barrel and the bearings for the two bolt guides. The bolt is of the rotating type with multi-lugs and this runs on the steel bolt guide rods which are held in the receiver.

(top) **An Austrian soldier mans a roadblock during a UN peacekeeping mission. He is carrying the Steyr AUG rifle.**

(bottom) **Members of the Austrian Army on exercise carrying the Steyr AUG rifle.**

This eliminates contact between the receiver and the bolt. The return springs are concealed in the guide rods, the left-hand one of which, along with the cocking handle, serves to cock the weapon for firing by operating the bolt when loading, whilst the right-hand rod acts as the gas piston. The barrel unit of the AUG comprises the barrel itself, the gas port and cylinder, the gas regulator and a folding handle, which can be used to change barrels when converting the weapon from one role to another. The barrel locks into the receiver by a series of interrupted lugs, and, once aligned properly, the gas cylinder, which carries a short-stroke piston, is lined up with the right-hand bolt guide rod. The safety catch is located at the top of the pistol grip and is ambidextrous in action.

The weapon features no fire selector switch and instead relies on trigger pressure to achieve selective fire. For single shots the first pressure is taken up to the first sear action. After releasing the trigger and applying further pressure fully automatic fire is achieved. The automatic firing lever will prevent firing until the bolt is locked. This action, it must be said, does take a little getting used to. However, once it has been mastered it comes as second nature.

(above) **Member of the Army of the Republic of Ireland in the doorway of an Alouette III helicopter. He is carrying the Steyr AUG rifle.**

(below) **The Steyr AUG fitted with the M203-type 40mm grenade launcher. Note separate trigger mechanism for firing the grenade.**

The weapon is supplied with ammunition from a 30-round capacity box magazine, and has a cyclic rate of 650 rounds per minute. However, to prevent the barrel from overheating too quickly the maximum number of rounds to be fired in full automatic is recommended as being no more than 150.

To field strip the AUG, the infantryman first checks that the weapon is in an unloaded and safe state. He then removes the barrel by pressing in the barrel locking stud with his thumb, and, using the handle, rotates it to the right until the lugs disengage and the barrel can be pulled forward. By turning the cocking handle to the left the bolt moves forward. The housing lock is pushed to the right until it engages and the housing group extracted through the butt, with the bolt assembly. The bolt assembly is removed from the housing group, the butt cap is depressed and the rear sling swivel, which acts as a securing pin, is removed from the left. The butt cap can then be removed and the removal of the trigger mechanism, by pulling it backwards from the butt, completes the stripping action. The infantryman need strip no further for normal field cleaning and servicing.

There are a number of other features and attachments which can be used with the AUG, such as rifle grenades, a knife-type bayonet and a blank firing attachment for training purposes. The rifle can also be fitted with a 40mm grenade launcher, which operates in a similar manner to the M203.

The AUG has been taken into service by various police forces around the world, as well as military units.

SPECIFICATIONS:

(Standard rifle version)

Calibre:	5.56mm x 45
Weight:	3.6kg
Length:	790mm
Barrel:	508mm
Rifling:	One turn in 228mm

(top) **The short-barrelled FN-FNC 5.56mm rifle as used by the Belgian Army.**

(middle) **The short-barrelled FN-FNC 5.56mm rifle as used by the Belgian Army.**

(bottom) **The standard FN-FNC 5.56mm rifle as used by the Belgian Army.**

The FNC assault rifle was introduced by the Belgian company, Fabrique Nationale of Herstal, and replaced the older Carabine Automatique Légère, or CAL, which had been produced by the same company. Fabrique Nationale, now a subsidiary of the French armaments company, GIAT, has produced many other weapons, including the FN-FAL which was taken into service by many countries. The Australians accepted the FN-FAL

The standard FN-FNC 5.56mm rifle as used by the Belgian Army.

into service as the L1A1, the Canadians knew it as the C1 and the British Army used a version known as the L1A1 self-loading rifle, all of which fired the 7.62mm x 51 cartridge.

The FNC assault rifle fires the smaller calibre 5.56mm x 45mm cartridge from a 30-round capacity magazine, with both military versions having a cyclic rate of fire of between 600 and 750 rounds per minute. The FNC can fire either the SS109 or M193 round, with only slight variation in muzzle velocity. The magazines used on the rifles are of the same type used by the M16, and can also be used on the Minimi light machine gun.

The two military versions are identical, except for the length of the barrel, and have folding butt stocks. There is the ability to fit reinforced polyamide butt stocks to the weapons as an optional feature, but the current trend appears to be for shorter rifles, which means designs with folding stocks are often adopted for service. There is a 'Law Enforcement' version of the FNC which differs from the two military versions only by having no three-round burst facility or the capability of firing fully automatic. Despite this, it can still fire at a cyclic rate of 60 rounds per minute, which should more than meet any law enforcement requirement.

The operation of the FNC is by gas, using the well-proven, almost standard, method of mounting the return piston and gas cylinder above the barrel. The breech is locked by a rotating bolt with a two-lug head, which locks into the barrel extension. This design reduces the stress on the bolt and bolt carrier, and so can be made much lighter. The overall weight of the weapon is kept to a minimum by manufacturing the body from pressed steel; the trigger frame is of light alloy and the forestock is plastic.

The rifles can be used either left or right handed and there is also the option of fitting a removable bipod to the standard, or long, version of the FNC. The sights on the weapons comprise an adjustable post-type for the front sight with a flip-type aperture rear sight, which has lateral adjustment for range settings. Most types of day and night sights can be fitted to the mounting bracket, provided they have NATO standard fittings. This may limit the range of optical devices capable of being used with the FNC, but it does eliminate the need to machine and fit special adapter brackets.

The fire selector switch is located on the left-hand side of the weapon, just above the trigger guard and features all the settings necessary, including fully automatic. The weapons are easy to field strip for cleaning and require no tools for this process. After unloading and making the weapon safe, the user pushes the body securing pin from the right-hand side, just above the pistol grip, and this releases the lower portion of the weapon to expose the working parts. Pulling the cocking handle back pulls the bolt assembly to the rear, where it can be withdrawn from the weapon.

The FNC rifles can be fitted with either the American-style M7 knife-type bayonet with an adapter bracket, or the tubular handled bayonet which was specially developed for the rifle and fits over the flash-hider. Unfortunately, this latter type of bayonet puts it in the same category as the British L85A1 bayonet and the bayonet fitted to the Swedish SG540 series of rifles, with its latent handling difficulties after firing. The FNC standard rifle can fire rifle grenades, for which purpose **13** the rifle is fitted with a gas-tap device that folds over the front sight and serves to prevent the flow of gas from the special ballistite cartridge from entering the cylinder. This device serves to give extra firing pressure to the rifle grenade and also acts as the sighting unit for the firer who aligns it along the upper surface of the grenade to gauge the best elevation for firing.

SPECIFICATIONS:

	Standard FNC	Short-barrelled FNC
Calibre:	5.56mm x 45 (SS109 or M193)	5.56mm x 45 (SS109 or M193)
Length:	997mm	911mm (Butt stock extended)
	766mm	666mm (Butt stock folded)
Weight:	3.8kg	3.7kg
Barrel:	449mm	363mm
Rifling:	Six grooves, right hand, one turn in 178mm	
Optional rifling:	Six grooves, right hand, one turn in 305mm	
Muzzle velocity:	965m/sec with M193 round	
	915m/sec with SS109 round	

The M76 assault rifle traces its origins back to the late 1950s, when Finland decided to produce a local copy of the Russian built AK47. The first model to be developed was known as the M60 and featured plastic furniture in place of wooden; the muzzle brake was also slightly different from the Russian model.

The M60 was taken into service by the Finnish armed forces and became known as the M62. This remained the standard weapon of Finland's armed forces until 1976, when the M76 rifle appeared. This was actually a marketing move to take advantage of the different calibres and styles beginning to emerge at that time. So successful was this relaunch of the basic weapon that the Finnish armed forces also picked it up.

The M76 is available in either the Standard or the Law Enforcement M76 models. Each of these is also available in the 7.62mm x 39 (the calibre used by the former Warsaw Pact states) or 5.56mm x 45, which is the NATO standard. Each of the designs comes in three variants: one with a standard folding butt stock; one with all-plastic stocks; and a version which has a plastic forestock but wooden butt stock. These are known respectively as M76T (which has a tubular-shaped butt stock), the M76F with a folding plastic butt stock, and the M76W to indicate it has a wooden butt stock. There is a long-barrelled version, known as the M78, which is fitted with a bipod, but this is more commonly used as a Light Support Weapon rather than as an assault rifle.

The frame of the M76 series is manufactured entirely from milled chrome-alloy steel, as is the mechanism. This produces a very hard-wearing weapon able to withstand the rigours of the battlefield and extremes in terrain and climate. The rifle can be field stripped without the use of tools, and breaks down into six component parts: the frame, top cover, bolt assembly and return spring assembly, gas tube and guide.

Each version of the M76 uses box magazines, with capacities of 15, 20 or 30 rounds, and can achieve cyclic rates of 600 to 650 rounds per minute. The fire selector

(top) **The M76 rifle as used by the Finnish Army. This version has the tubular folding butt stock.**

(bottom) **M76 rifle with fixed wooden butt stock, as used by the Finnish Army.**

The Finnish M76 rifle stripped for cleaning. Note the cleaning kit, knife-type bayonet and the 20- and 30-round capacity magazines.

switch is located on the right-hand side of the weapon, along with the cocking handle, and has three settings. The top setting is 'safe', the middle setting allows a three-round burst, and the lower setting is for single shot. This configuration of cocking lever and fire selector might appear to be awkward, but they can be operated quite easily by right-or left-handed firers. However, the idea of a reciprocating cocking handle coming so close to the user's face could be unnerving for first-time firers of this weapon.

The M76T carries a cleaning kit – comprising a three-piece barrel rod, barrel brushes, screwdriver and oil bottle – inside the tubular frame of the butt stock. A knife-type bayonet can be fitted to each version of the M76. The foresight of the rifle is protected by a tunnel guard and is fully adjustable. The rear sight is of the folding-leaf type with peep-sight blade, and is graduated in 100m increments out to 600m range. For use in low light level conditions the sights can be turned inwards to expose illuminated surfaces to the firer who can use them to align on a target. This is not the most accurate means of engaging a target in darkening conditions, but is a good deal better than nothing at all.

SPECIFICATIONS:

Calibre:	5.56mm x 45 NATO
	7.62mm x 39 Russian/CIS
Weight empty:	3.9kg
Weight loaded:	4.520kg with 30-round magazine of 5.56mm
	4.910kg with 30-round magazine of 7.62mm
Length:	950mm (butt stock extended)
	710mm (butt stock folded)
Barrel:	420mm
Rifling:	Six grooves, right hand, one turn in 300mm (5.56mm)
	Four grooves, right hand, one turn in 250mm (7.62mm)
Muzzle velocity:	900m/sec (5.56mm)
	719m/sec (7.62mm)

The French Army's FAMAS, standing for Fusil Automatique, Manufacture d'Armes St Etienne, is known as the 'Bugle' because of its unusual profile. The distinctive long carrying handle, which also incorporates the sights, makes this bullpup weapon immediately recognisable. Since the end of 1979 the FAMAS has been used to arm the French armed forces, and to cope with the throughput of conscript servicemen the French armed forces have ordered some 700,000 units of this weapon. It is made all the more distinctive by the fact that it is entirely black in colour.

The FAMAS can fire in single or semi-automatic fire mode, three-round burst and fully automatic. It has two fire selector switches to allow these operations. First is the semi-automatic mode, and the switch for this setting is located at the trigger level. By setting this to position

'1' the other two modes of firing are rendered inoperative. Second is the three-round burst selector which is located on the underside of the mechanism unit. When the setting of '3' is selected the fully automatic mode is inoperative and conversely, when the 'R' for automatic mode is selected, the other firing functions are inoperative.

The FAMAS rifle fires standard 5.56mm x 45mm NATO rounds from box magazines with either a 20- or 30-round capacity, and has a cyclic rate between 1,000 and 1,100 rounds per minute. By pulling the trigger in the semi-automatic mode the connecting rod causes rotation of the sear drive, which in turn frees the hammer. Under the action of the hammer spring, the hammer rotates forward to strike the firing pin which hits the base of the round in the chamber and the weapon is fired. The hammer is recocked during the backward movement of the bolt and at the end of the stroke the hammer once more hooks onto the automatic sear. During the

(left) **The FAMAS 5.56mm rifle as used by the French Army. Note the cocking handle located under the carrying handle.**

(below) **Members of a French artillery unit equipped with the FAMAS. Note how the sling allows the crew to serve the gun with the need to put the weapon on the ground.**

automatic mode the firing sequence is virtually the same, except that the hammer does not engage with the driven sear and fires as soon as the automatic sear is clear.

The three-round burst facility of the FAMAS is slightly more complicated. When the limiter is engaged and the trigger pulled, on each backward rotation of the hammer, the hammer rod in turn causes rotation of the limiter operating lever and the driving pawl. This causes the ratchet wheel to make one turn corresponding to the counting of the shot. The first round is counted when the hammer is released to strike the firing pin and its rod frees the operating lever, which returns to its original position supported on the hub of the ratchet wheel. On the third round being fired the limiter catch stops the hammer at the end of its backward movement, hooking it onto the lower catch of the hammer. This hooking is achieved by rotation of the ratchet wheel cam, which on the third shot causes the limiter catch to pivot. Firing is interrupted and when pressure is released from the trigger it releases the limiter catch in two stages.

The FAMAS was not in service in time to equip French troops going into Kolwezi in May 1978. However, it was much in evidence during the Gulf War of 1990–91

(above) **Soldiers of the French Army crew a Milan anti-tank missile. The man standing is carrying the FAMAS rifle slung across his chest to allow him to perform other tasks.**

(below) **Two French mortar men with a FAMAS rifle.**

when it was used by the French contingent which made up part of the Coalition Forces facing Saddam Hussein's Iraqi troops during Operation DESERT STORM.

The FAMAS is one of only three proven bullpup rifle designs in current use. It can fire a wide choice of rifle grenades, including anti-personnel, illuminating and anti-tank. The firer can adopt any one of three firing positions when using rifle grenades from the FAMAS. Firstly he can adopt the prone position with the butt stock resting on the ground and the weapon either at the high angle, 75°, or low angle, 45°, to engage the target. These angles will allow the firer to engage targets between 140m to 360m and 70m to 180m respectively. The firing selector is always set in position '1' when firing rifle grenades. The firer can either stand or kneel to fire his weapon from the shoulder in the direct firing mode in which case he can quite easily engage moving targets out to ranges of 75m to 100m. The last method of firing rifle grenades from the FAMAS is to use the weapon's integral bipod for support and fire in the prone position.

The FAMAS will function in temperatures ranging from -40°C to +51.5°C, but when firing rifle grenades the lower end of operating temperatures fall off to -31.5°C. It is recommended that no more than four full magazines be fired through the FAMAS without allowing some time to cool down. Barrel life of the FAMAS is put at 10,000 rounds and 420 rifle grenade firings.

The FAMAS fires the SS109 5.56mm standard NATO round which will penetrate 3.5mm of mild steel plate at 625m range and 7mm of armour plate and 15mm of light alloy plate at 180m and 273m range respectively.

The magazine is inserted into the magazine well located behind the pistol grip and the cocking lever is mounted on the upper surface of the weapon's body and protected by the carrying handle. In fact, a warning instruction in the weapon handling manual warns against the firer putting his hand between the protective/carrying handle and the cocking lever slot during firing.

The FAMAS can be easily stripped for field cleaning without the use of tools. Firstly, the weapon is unloaded and cleared as being 'safe to handle' with the magazine removed. The locking for the butt stock assembly is removed, which allows this unit to be lifted. Removing the assembly pin on the protective handle allows this unit to be lifted clear and the butt assembly is stripped. The mechanism assembly stud is next removed, usually

pushed out of place with the tip of a bullet, and this permits the mechanism to be rotated and lifted clear of the body. By pulling back on the cocking lever the internal working parts of the rifle are removed.

The FAMAS has been evaluated by some overseas countries, but as far as this author is aware few if any sales have been made. That is not to say that potential customers are not happy with the weapon, merely that they are satisfied with the weapons they currently have in service.

The author has fired the FAMAS on a number of occasions, and found it to be a comfortable weapon, easy to control and with good handling.

There is a training system developed specially for the FAMAS which allows it to be fired on an indoor range, using compressed air to fire pellets on semi-automatic. This is a training aid which allows service personnel to become familiarised with the workings of the weapon before moving on to the outdoor range and 'live' ammunition.

The rifle is capable of having a knife-type bayonet mounted and a special 'universal' sling allows the weapon to be carried in several ways and still leave the user's hands free to complete other tasks. The FAMAS is currently in service with several French law enforcement agencies such as the Gendarmerie, as well as the French armed forces.

SPECIFICATIONS:

Calibre:	5.56mm x 45mm
Weight:	3.610kg (without attachments)
Length:	757mm overall
Barrel:	488mm
Rifling:	Three grooves, right hand, one turn in 305mm
	Three grooves, right hand, one turn in 228mm
Muzzle velocity: 960m/sec	

The German-designed Gewehr 3 rifle, or G3, is one of the most widely used weapons of its type in the world, being exported to five continents and built under licence in a number of countries. It is available in either 7.62mm or 5.56mm calibre. Among the many countries to use the G3 rifle are Turkey, Norway, Chad, Guyana and Pakistan; the latter also produces Heckler and Koch weapons under licence.

The basic G3 design is now quite old, but that is not to say that it has passed its usefulness as a frontline service weapon. Quite the contrary as many, even early examples, are still in use around the world. The standard model of the rifle is known as the G3A3, which was preceded by four models including the prototype, and this has a plastic forestock and butt stock. The G3A3 ZF is the version with a telescopic sight fitted and the G3A4 is the version fitted with a retractable butt stock. The Turkish defence company of Makina ve Kimya Endustrisi Kurumu manufactures the G3 rifle in 7.62mm calibre under licence in both the fixed and retractable butt stock versions.

The weapon uses the standard Heckler and Koch delayed blowback design, using rollers as the method of delay. It has selective fire settings, including the usual safety setting, for either semi- or fully automatic fire with a cyclic rate of 600 rounds per minute, fed from a detachable 20-round box magazine. The weapon can be used to launch a whole range of rifle grenades either of the 'bullet trap' design or the type requiring ballistite cartridges. All types of rifle grenades can be fired from the G3, providing they have an internal tail diameter of 22mm.

When firing a grenade requiring a ballistite cartridge to launch it, the magazine is removed and a special blank cartridge is inserted. The firer can then engage targets out to 100m with some degree of accuracy. With the

The H&K G3 rifle fitted with an early small arms fire simulator, the SIMGUN. The small box fitted to the muzzle of the weapon emits a low-level, eye-safe, laser to simulate firing the weapon when blank rounds are used. Note the firer is wearing a receiver harness and has sensors on his helmet. These record a near miss or direct hit, activating an audible signal to warn the infantryman that he has been 'hit'.

(top) **Members of the newly-formed Franco-German brigade deploying from a helicopter. These are German troops and are carrying the G3 rifle.**

(bottom) **The H&K G3 rifle in its standard form seen from the left. Note the fire selector switch just above the pistol grip.**

'bullet trap' type rifle grenades the projectile is simply placed over the muzzle of the barrel and a standard ball round fired. Baffles inside the tail of the rifle grenade collapse as the round passes through them and the kinetic energy imparted propels the grenade. Rifle grenades are seen as allowing an infantryman to engage targets which are at ranges too far to be engaged with

hand grenades and too close for light mortars of 51mm and 60mm calibres.

The popularity of 40mm grenade launchers fitted under the weapon, in the manner of the M203 on the M16 rifle, has led to the development of a similar device for the G3. Although 40mm grenade launchers on weapons such as the G3 are becoming more popular, it is unlikely that they will ever replace the rifle grenade completely.

A sub-calibre training system using .22 inch rounds (5.6mm x 16mm) is available to familiarise troops with the handling and functioning details of the G3 at a fraction of the cost of normal rounds. To convert the rifle to .22 training roles, a sub-calibre insert is slid into the barrel and fixed into position with pins; a special bolt and magazine are also used in place of the normal components. The magazine holds 20 rounds of .22 ammunition. This conversion allows troops to be trained on indoor ranges to acquire their battlefield skills in weapon handling and target engagement. The training system can be used before allowing troops to use full-bore calibres or as an all-weather aid.

For field training exercises the G3 can be fitted with a special 'blank firing adapter' which allows the weapon to be used in a realistic manner but only firing blank rounds. This allows troops to engage in large-scale training manoeuvres in complete safety.

To field strip the G3 the magazine is first removed and the cocking lever worked to ensure the chamber is empty. Two locking pins which secure the back plate are removed and the butt stock can be removed. By pushing out the single pin which holds the pistol grip, the trigger assembly is stripped out. Working the cocking handle once more allows the bolt assembly to be removed from the main body of the weapon, and this too can be stripped for cleaning.

The G3 is fitted with a post-type front sight and an adjustable rear sight which has a 'U' shaped battle setting and apertures with 100m increments out to 400m range. Trigger pull on the G3 can be set to between 3.6 and 4.1 kg. The G3A3 and G3A4 versions have components

which are interchangeable to increase commonality and reduce stock holding of spare parts.

Specifications of the G3 built under licence do not vary all that much from the original Heckler and Koch design, but for the purposes of this entry the specifications of the Turkish G3A3 and G3A4 are used.

SPECIFICATIONS:

Calibre:	7.62mm x 51mm
Weight:	4.40kg (G3A3 unloaded)
Weight:	4.70kg (G3A4 unloaded)
Length:	1,020mm (G3A3)
Length (G3A4):	1,020mm (butt stock extended)
	840mm (butt stock retracted)
Barrel:	450mm
Rifling:	Four grooves, right hand, one turn in 305mm
Muzzle velocity:	800m/sec

German troops of the newly-formed Franco-German brigade deploy from an APC, carrying the H&K G3 rifle.

The German HK33E rifle designed by Heckler and Koch is unarguably one of the most versatile rifles to enter military service. There are five variants of the rifle, with the basic HK33E capable of being configured as a sniping rifle; it can also be fitted with an HK79 launcher to fire 40mm grenades, in the same manner as the M203 fitted to the M16A2.

The variants of the HK33E include models with fixed or retractable butt stocks, a rifle with bipod, the sniper version with telescopic sight, and the HK33EK, which is a shorter carbine version. The rifle fires the standard NATO 5.56mm x 45 round, with a cyclic rate of 750 rounds per minute. The rifle, which is basically a scaled-down version of the more powerful G3 rifle, uses the same delayed blowback system as the G3, firing from a closed breech.

The bolt comprises two main parts, with the bolt-head containing two rollers which are forced out into recesses in the barrel extension by angled faces on the bolt-body. When the weapon is fired, the gas pressure exerts force onto the bolt-face to drive it back, but the rollers have to move inwards before the bolt-head can move. The recesses are shaped to permit the slight rearward movement of the rollers to force them inwards. The mass of the bolt-body resists this movement, as does the force of the return spring, transmitted to the rollers by way of the angled faces lying between them. The bolt-body moves back four times the length of the bolt-face as the angled faces drive rearwards; at the same time the rollers move inwards. Once the rollers are clear of the recesses in the barrel extension the remaining gas pressure in the chamber forces the two parts of the block back together, but the two parts are still displaced relatively by the rollers. The bolt-face holds the cartridge and after firing the spent case strikes the ejector and it is thrown out to the right-hand side of the weapon.

The barrel of the HK33E is chrome-plated to ensure long service life and is capable of accepting bayonets and of firing rifle grenades directly from the muzzle. The plastic stock of the rifle can be moulded in camouflage forms, including desert, jungle and standard drab green. The trigger assembly of the HK33E is virtually identical to the G3 and the ambidextrous fire selector switch allows the weapon to be fired in either single-shot, three-round burst or fully automatic modes.

The basic sights have a V-shaped rear sight for a battle setting, and other settings are marked at increments of 100m out to 400m range. The HK33E will accept various optical units including night-vision equipment. There is a separate unit, the HK79A1, which fires the 40mm x 46mm grenade. With this fitted the firer can engage targets out to 350m with no degradation in the overall performance of the rifle itself. The 40mm grenade-launcher unit can be fitted to the rifle, in place of the handguard, without the aid of tools. This device, which weighs only 1.4kg, can be fitted to all versions of the HK33E, including the carbine version.

An interesting novelty is the fact that the field cleaning kit for the HK33E, which includes barrel brushes and pull-through, is contained in the pistol grip.

The H&K 33E rifle seen from the left-hand side. Note the cocking handle on the forestock, just behind the front sight, the magazine release catch in front of the trigger guard, and the fire selector switch.

SPECIFICATIONS:

Calibre:	5.56mm x 45 NATO
Weight:	3.90kg
Weight:	3.95kg (with retractable butt stock)
Length:	920mm (with fixed butt stock)
	740mm (with retractable butt stock collapsed)
	670mm (HK33EK with retractable butt stock collapsed)
Barrel length:	410mm (HK33E without flash suppressor)
	340mm (HK33EK without flash suppressor)
Rifling:	Six grooves, right hand, one turn in 178mm
Muzzle velocity:	900m/sec (HK33E)
	850m/sec (HK33EK)

The German-built Heckler and Koch HK53 was designed along the functional lines of the G3 assault rifle, which is also manufactured by Heckler and Koch. Although the HK53 has the appearance of a sub-machine gun, the fact that it fires a cartridge of 5.56mm x 45mm NATO standard puts it very firmly in the category of assault rifle. The company of Heckler and Koch cite that it is a sub-machine gun with the performance of an assault rifle, but all weapon encyclopaedias list the weapon in the category of rifles, including the eminent Jane's *Infantry Weapons*.

The HK53 features a recoil-operated roller-locked bolt system firing from the closed and locked position, which adds to the weapon's accuracy when firing the first round. The rollers delay the rearward motion of the breech-head until the pressure has dropped sufficiently to permit the breech-block to be blown back in safety. The weapon has a cyclic rate of 700 rounds per minute and settings, including 'safe', which permit the firer to operate the HK53 in semi-automatic, three-round burst or fully automatic roles. The fire selector switch is ambidextrous to allow for left-handed users or tactical requirements when firing from behind cover. The trigger mechanism of the HK53 is incorporated into the weapon's pistol grip and is identical to that fitted to the G3 rifle, a weapon of which it may be considered as a scaled-down version.

The barrel of the HK53 is cold-forged and free-floating, which means it does not come into contact with the receiver over its full length. Indeed, there is no change in point of impact when it has heated up even after prolonged firing.

The weapon can easily be stripped down into its sub-assemblies without tools for the purposes of cleaning and basic field maintenance. An extendable butt stock is featured to allow troops operating from APCs and helicopters to use it without snagging. The HK53 is capable of mounting a series of optical sights, including 4x24 telescopic sights and aiming-point projectors for accuracy when engaged in close-quarter actions, such as hostage situations. Unlike most standard assault rifle designs, the HK53 does not have the length to permit a 40mm grenade launcher to be mounted under the body, nor can standard rifle grenades be launched from the muzzle of the barrel. Despite that, it remains a functional weapon which has seen much service with police and some special military units. The foresight of the weapon is of the post-type and the rear sight has settings in 100m increments from 100m to 400m, and a 390mm sighting radius. The HK53 uses either 25- or 30-round capacity magazines.

The HK53 is classified as an assault rifle as it fires a 5.56mm rifle cartridge. However, due to its compact size it can serve in the role of an SMG. Note the position of the cocking handle, just behind the front sight, and the collapsible butt stock.

SPECIFICATIONS:

Calibre: 5.56mm x 45mm

Weight: 3.05kg (unloaded)

                  3.65kg (with loaded 25-round magazine)

Length: 780mm (butt stock extended)

                  590mm (butt stock retracted)

Barrel length: 211mm

Rifling: Six grooves, right hand, one twist in 178mm

Muzzle velocity: 735m/sec

Israeli servicemen carrying the Short Assault Rifle (SAR) version of the Galil.

Israeli tank crew armed with the SAR version of the Galil.

The origins of the Galil are well-documented, but to recap briefly it was designed by Israel Galil and Yaacov Lior, being heavily influenced by the rugged Kalashnikov AK47 design. The Israelis decided to rearm with 5.56mm calibre weapons after the Six Day War in 1967 a number of weapons using this calibre were brought in for trials, but these were unsuccessful. The design put forward by the team of Galil and Lior was chosen for adoption in 1972, because it was deemed to be the weapon which best suited the requirements of the Israeli armed forces.

The Galil rifle was first issued to Israeli troops in the 5.56mm calibre in 1973, but it is currently available in two calibres: 5.56mm x 45 and 7.62mm x 51. There are several variants on the basic Galil design, including the sniping version (qv), and these have in turn influenced the development of the South African R4 rifle.

Apart from the sniping version, all variants of the Galil feature a folding metal-framed butt stock, including the ARM which has an integral bipod, that doubles as a useful set of wirecutters, and allows the weapon to be used in the Light Support Weapon role. The Galil is of conventional layout, with the magazine in front of the

pistol grip, and the cyclic rate for the ARM is 650 rounds per minute, whilst for the SAR, or Short Assault Rifle, the cyclic rate is 750 rounds per minute. The effective ranges for these weapons are 600m and 550m respectively.

There are three types of 5.56mm magazine available for use with the Galil. One has a 35-round capacity and another a 50-round capacity, which is particularly useful with the ARM version. The third type of magazine bears a white stripe to indicate that it is pre-loaded with ballistite cartridges for use when firing rifle grenades. In the 7.62 version the Galil uses a 25-round capacity magazine, with a 12-round capacity magazine also bearing the white stripe to indicate ballistite cartridges for rifle grenades. The Galil can be used to launch all types of rifle grenade, including anti-tank, anti-personnel, illuminating and smoke.

The Galil is gas-operated and functions on the rotating bolt locking system with selective fire, but no gas regulator. Instead, the gas block is pinned to the barrel and the gas track drilled back at 30 degrees into the gas cylinder. The piston rod and shank are both chrome-plated for durability and the bolt carrier forms an extension to the piston end. This is hollowed out over the bolt to accept the return spring.

The Galil fires from the closed bolt position and the cocking handle is attached to this to give a positive action for bolt closure. The cocking handle is angled upwards to allow the firer to cock the weapon with either hand.

The fire selector switch is located on the left hand side of the weapon by the trigger guard, and the magazine release catch is positioned just in front of the trigger guard, allowing the firer to change magazines with the minimum of lost time. The Galil is fitted with a post-type front sight protected by a short tube, as featured on the Finnish M76 and the German G3 rifles. The rear sight is of the flip-type with settings between 300m and 500m and a tritium night sight, which is separate from the daytime sight.

The Galil breaks down into six component parts for field cleaning. As with other rifles, the magazine is first removed and the weapon checked to ensure that there is no chambered round. Once it has been declared safe to handle, the guide rod of the return spring is pushed forward and the cover of the receiver is lifted off. The return rod and spring are removed. The cocking handle is withdrawn and the bolt is lifted clear of the receiver and rotated out of the carrier.

The ARM version also features a folding-type carrying handle, but the SAR version does not have this, nor does the standard AR (Assault Rifle) version.

The Galil is in use with the Israeli Defence Forces, and some numbers have been sold abroad. The Galil has been extensively used by Israeli forces in combat situations, where it has given good account of itself and has been proven to be a rugged design capable of absorbing punishing handling in even the harshest of conditions.

SPECIFICATIONS:

	5.56mm version	7.62mm version
Weight:	4.35kg (ARM with bipod and carrying handle)	4.0kg (ARM minus bipod and carrying handle)
	3.95kg (AR)	3.95kg (AR)
	3.75kg (SAR)	3.75kg (SAR)
Length:	979mm (ARM/AR with butt stock extended)	1,050mm (ARM/AR with butt stock extended)
	840mm (SAR with butt stock extended)	915mm (SAR with butt stock extended)
	742mm (ARM/AR with butt stock folded)	810mm (ARM/AR with butt stock folded)
	614mm (SAR with butt stock folded)	675mm (SAR with butt stock folded)
Barrel:	460mm (ARM/AR)	535mm (ARM/AR)
	332mm (SAR)	400mm (SAR)
Rifling:	Six grooves, right hand, one turn in 305mm	Four grooves, right hand, one turn in 305mm
Muzzle velocity:	950m/sec (ARM/AR)	850m/sec (ARM/AR)
	900m/sec (SAR)	800m/sec (SAR)

The Italian Army accepted the Beretta 70/90 assault rifle series into service in July 1990 to replace the older AR70/223 rifle, of which it is an improved version. The 70/90 series is made up of five weapons, all of which fire the 5.56mm x 45 cartridge. First is the standard AR70/90 which is for use by the ordinary infantryman. The SC70/90 is the carbine version of the weapon and is intended for use by special forces units. The SCS70/90 is the special carbine, short, for use by drivers and armoured troops. The SCP70/90 and AS70/90 are versions equipped with a grenade-launcher attachment and the light support weapon respectively.

The AR70/90 uses a 30-round capacity box magazine and the weapon has a cyclic rate of 680 rounds per minute. The magazine well has been designed to allow the weapon range to utilise the M16 type magazine. The magazine release catch can be operated by either hand and is located by the magazine housing. The SC version has a comparable cyclic rate to the AR, but the SCS version is set at 670 rounds per minute.

All the 70/90 series fire from the closed bolt position. The receiver of the weapon series is trapezoidal in section, with steel bolt guide rods welded in place, and uses a gas piston mounted over the barrel to actuate the bolt carrier and two-lug rotating bolt. All weapons in the series feature a detachable carrying handle which is removed when telescopic sights or night vision units are to be fitted. The carrying handle contains a luminescent light source as an aiming aid in low light conditions. The normal rear sight on the AR70/90 rifle is a two-position unit which is adjustable for windage and has apertures for 250m and 400m ranges. The front sight is of the normal blade-type.

The trigger mechanism can be altered to suit a

The 70/90 range of Italian weapons known as the AR, SC and SCS.

variety of functions. In the basic version the rifle can fire single rounds, three-round bursts or fully automatic. However, a system to restrict the action to single and three-round burst only is available. Likewise, the three-round bursts can be removed, leaving the weapon to function in either semi- or fully automatic fire only. The trigger guard can be rotated and placed alongside the pistol grip to allow the firer to use the weapon unrestricted when wearing gloves or mittens in subzero conditions. The gas cylinder has three settings, one for normal use, the second for use in adverse conditions and the last setting is closed for use when firing rifle grenades. The regulator is provided with an aiming device for use with rifle grenades and this impinges on the normal line of sight to give the firer a visual indication that it is set. In the normal, or lowered, setting this lever serves to prevent the firer from trying to load a rifle grenade with it in the wrong setting.

The 70/90 series can be fitted with a bayonet and the cleaning kit is carried in the base of the pistol grip. The AR70/90 rifle has a fixed butt stock but the SC and SCS versions both have folding butt stocks which collapse forward along the right-hand side of the weapon. The cocking handle is on the right-hand side of the weapon and can be operated by either hand.

SPECIFICATIONS:

	AR70/90	SC70/90	SCS70/90
Length:	998mm	986mm	876mm
	–	751mm (with butt stock folded)	647mm (with butt stock folded)
Barrel length:	450mm	450mm	352mm
Weight:	3.990kg	3.990kg	3.790kg
Rifling:	Six grooves, right hand, one turn in 178mm (all versions)		

The Type 64 rifle is used only by the Japanese Self-Defense Forces and was chosen for introduction into service following trials and field tests involving several weapon designs. The weapon fires the standard 7.62mm x 51mm NATO round, but with the propellant charge reduced by ten per cent, which produces a reduced muzzle impulse and recoil force to the firer. This limiting of the charge was due to the small physical stature of Japanese troops.

The Type 64 can fire the full charge NATO round, but it is necessary for the gas regulator to be adjusted so that the pressure of the gases reaching the piston head is reduced. The gas regulator, which controls the flow of gas to the gas cylinder and piston located above the barrel, has three port settings, and can be shut off completely to allow the Type 64 to fire rifle grenades.

The Type 64 is fed by a detachable box-type magazine which contains 20 rounds, and is conventional in appearance. The magazine is inserted into the magazine well under the body of the weapon and the release catch is located directly behind it.

The rifle, which was designed by General K Iwashita, uses the tilting block system as the method of locking. In action the block is lifted into engagement, after which it is lowered and carried back by the bolt carrier. The rifle has a cyclic rate of 500 rounds per minute, with a claimed effective range of 400m, and to assist in accuracy it is fitted with a bipod to the fore-end. The butt stock is fixed and of the straight-through design. The weapon has not been produced for the Japanese Self-Defense Force since 1990, but it is still in current use.

SPECIFICATIONS:

Calibre:	7.62 x 51 (reduced load)
Weight:	4.4kg (empty)
Length:	990mm
Length of barrel:	450mm
Rifling:	Four grooves, right hand, one turn in 250mm
Muzzle velocity:	700m/sec (reduced charge)
	800m/sec (full charge)

The Japanese Type 64 rifle which fires a cartridge with a reduced charge. This is being replaced in service by the lighter, more compact Type 89 rifle.

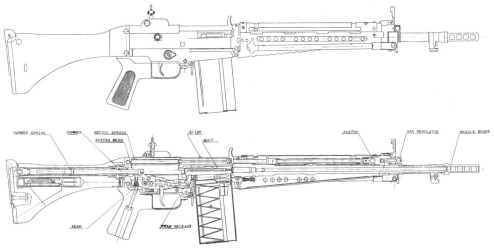

7·62 mm Type 64 rifle

Following the trend favoured by other armed forces, the Japanese Self-Defense Force has introduced the Type 89 rifle which fires the smaller 5.56mm x 45mm round. Manufactured by Howa Machinery Ltd, who also manufactured the Type 64 rifle, this new rifle was developed with the co-operation of the Technical Research and Development Institute of the Japanese Defense Agency.

This is a typical assault rifle design and is available in two forms: one with a folding butt stock; the other with a fixed butt stock. Both also feature an integral bipod fitted to the fore-end. The rifle is operated by the usual method of gas being ported off into the gas chamber mounted above the barrel.

The design is unusual in that the piston rod in the long gas expansion chamber is stepped – the front diameter of the rod is smaller than at the rear, and it is positioned some way back from the gas port. Gas is ported into the gas chamber, where it rapidly expands, and the piston moves the bolt carrier with a light flick. This increases the functional reliability and service life of the moving parts. The breech mechanism of the Type 89 is locked by a rotating bolt, which has a seven-lug head locking into the barrel extension.

The rifle uses either a 20- or 30-round detachable box magazine, and has a cyclic rate of between 650 RPM and 850 RPM. The rifle has a three-round burst facility in the form of a detachable device located at the rear of the trigger housing, which is separated from the trigger mechanism for semi- and fully automatic firing.

The rear sight is of the aperture-type, fully adjustable for elevation and windage, and is fitted with a ballistic cam. The front sight is of the square post-type and is also fully adjustable. In use the sight radius is 440mm.

SPECIFICATIONS:

Calibre:	5.56mm x 45mm
Weight:	3.5kg
Length:	916mm (butt stock extended)
	670mm (butt stock folded)
Barrel length:	420mm
Rifling:	Six grooves, right hand, one turn in 178mm
Muzzle velocity:	920m/sec

Japanese troops, armed with the Type 89 rifle, being transported by a UH-1B helicopter. The Japanese Type 89 rifle fires the 5.56mm x 45 round and is lighter and more compact than the older Type 64 rifle which it is replacing.

The South Korean K2 rifle fitted with the M203-type 40mm grenade launcher.

The industrial manufacturing base in South Korea continues to grow stronger. Developing an armaments industry to compete in an already crowded and highly competitive market is risky, but the Pusan-based company of Daewoo Precision Industries Ltd has successfully developed the K2 assault rifle for the South Korean Army.

The K2 fires the standard 5.56mm round. At first glance the K2 is similar to the Colt 'Commando' rifle, but closer inspection reveals that the design has taken the best features from the M16, the AK47 and even the FN-FNC to produce a reliable and robust weapon. There are two versions of the K2. The standard assault rifle has a solid butt stock that folds forward and lies alongside the right-hand side of the receiver, and is locked in place with a system similar to the FN-FNC weapon. The second version of the K2 is a carbine, which has a collapsible wire and plastic butt stock and has a much shortened barrel.

Both versions are gas-operated with selective fire, including a three-round burst capability. The K2 uses standard M16-type magazines containing 30 rounds, and

South Korean troops carrying the K2 assault rifle on an assault training course.

can fire either M193 or SS109 5.56mm calibre rounds. The K2 uses the long-stroke piston, associated with the AK47, to operate a rotating bolt. The upper and lower receivers, manufactured from aluminium alloy forgings, give the rifle the appearance of the M16, but despite this there is no commonality and parts are not interchangeable between the two weapons.

The three-round burst cycle does not reset when the trigger is released and, instead, continues to fire from the cycle setting when the trigger is pulled for a second time. In other words, if the firer has fired only two rounds previously before releasing the trigger in the three-round burst setting, on pulling the trigger a second time he will fire only one round. Releasing the trigger again will put the sequence back into cycle once more.

The barrel is fitted with a muzzle brake/compensator which is designed with the ports to vent to the side and upwards. This action reduces the tendency for muzzle climb on this rather short weapon when it is fired on fully automatic.

The weapon is fitted with flip-over type rear sights, which offer either a small aperture for precise target engagement, or two illuminated dots for use in low light levels. The front sight of the carbine version is protected by blades and on the longer assault rifle version is protected by a tunnel-shaped device as fitted to the AK47. The front sight has an illuminated dot on one side

(above) **South Korean troops carrying the K2 assault rifle, a locally-produced weapon.**

(below) **South Korean troops listen to a lecture in the field. They are carrying their K2 assault rifles slung over their shoulders. Note the folding butt stock.**

to allow the firer to line up on his target in low light conditions. The sights for the K2 are graduated out to 600m range, but it is unlikely that an ordinary infantryman using this weapon would ever engage a target at such ranges with ordinary sights.

The K2 can be fitted with an M203-type 40mm grenade launcher, to allow infantrymen to engage targets with indirect fire using explosive projectiles, in the same way as with the M16 rifle.

SPECIFICATIONS:

Calibre:	5.56mm x 45mm; either M193 or SS109
Weight:	3.26kg (unloaded)
Length:	990mm (butt stock extended)
	730mm (butt stock collapsed)
Barrel:	465mm (without muzzle brake/compensator)
Rifling:	Six grooves, right hand
Muzzle velocity:	960m/sec (M193)
	920m/sec (SS109)

The South African-developed 40mm grenade launcher seen here fitted to the muzzle of an AK47 Russian-developed rifle. Note the front sight of the weapon which is well protected by the tube-like fitting.

The Russian-designed AK47 assault rifle is instantly recognisable to many people, due to its high profile in news footage, newspaper features and numerous magazine articles. It is also associated as being the favoured weapon of terrorists and guerrilla forces, from the Philippines to Northern Ireland, the Middle East and South America. It is more commonly referred to simply as the 'Kalashnikov', after the Russian designer Mikhail Kalashnikov who conceived the idea for the weapon in 1947. The weapon entered service in 1951, becoming

the standard rifle of the Russian Army in 1957, and is seen in many quarters as being the benchmark for the development of all current assault rifles.

The AK, or Avtomat Kalashnikova, is the success story of small arms history and has appeared in many shapes and forms. Indeed, most of the former member states of the Warsaw Pact had their own variation of the rifle, which they invariably built under licence from the former Russian State Factory Arsenals. For example, a Polish version, known as the PMK-DGN-60, featured a rifle grenade launcher, the LON-1, on the muzzle and had a fixed wooden butt stock. The Bulgarian Army used a standard version of the AK47 with a fixed wooden butt stock, but some models lacked an integral cleaning rod and bayonet lug. The Romanian AKM version had a forward pistol grip with fixed wooden butt stock, but the former East German Army was issued with the MPiKM version which had a fixed plastic butt stock with a wooden forestock. The Chinese produced their own version of the AK47, known as the Type 56, and this appeared in various forms, including a design which incorporated a fixed bayonet which folded back along the length of the forestock. Other designs of the Type 56 had either a

Russian infantry assault forward from their BMP armoured personnel carrier. They are carrying the AK47 assault rifle.

folding butt stock or fixed wooden butt stock.

It has been estimated that more than 35 million Kalashnikovs had been produced as early as the mid-1970s. Today that number could be doubled, when one takes into account the fact that Iraq produces its own version along with several other major producers, including North Korea which manufactures it as the Type 68.

The AK47 fires the 7.62mm x 39 round, which is a standard Russian-influenced calibre, from 30-round capacity magazines, and has a cyclic rate in the order of 600 rounds per minute. The function of this rifle is well known but, to recap very briefly, it is a gas-operated weapon having the gas piston rod permanently attached to the bolt carrier. A cam-track on the carrier rotates the bolt to lock, and, during the rearward stroke, the hammer is also cocked. The AK47 is laid out in a standard assault rifle design, with the magazine being located in front of the pistol grip. The cocking lever is fixed and moves with the action of the bolt during firing. This has the benefit of acting as a lever to close the bolt, should it not

close properly, to cycle the round during the firing sequence.

The AK47 is manufactured using a combination of pressed parts and machined parts. Parts machined from solid steel are used where extra strength is required. The barrel itself is chrome-plated for increased service life. This robust construction has produced a weapon which can function under the most arduous of conditions, from hot desert terrain to the subzero climates found in the mountainous regions of the Afghan hills.

The AK47 field strips into several parts, including the magazine, very quickly and without the need for tools. Once the magazine has been removed and the weapon cleared to ensure it is unloaded, the end of the return spring guide is pressed into the rear end of the receiver cover, which releases the cover from the receiver. The return spring guide is pushed forward to release it from

A version of the AK47 with a fixed wooden stock. It is seen here being trialled with an optical sight unit which has been developed in Western Europe.

its housing and allow it to be removed from the weapon. By pulling the cocking handle to the rear, the bolt carrier and bolt are moved back and removed from the weapon. This assembly can then be stripped further. By rotating the gas cylinder lock the gas cylinder is freed along with the upper hand guard. Unlike some Western designs, there are no small parts or pins to lose in the debris of a battlefield.

The basic Russian AK47 can be fitted with a knife-type bayonet but others, such as the Chinese Type 56, have a folding spike-type bayonet. The AKM rifle is the upgraded version of the original AK47 with several distinguishing features. For example, there is a groove on the lower hand-guard for the firer's fingers, the bayonet lug is under the gas-tap off point, a small compensator is fitted and the receiver cover has transverse ribs. The cyclic rate of fire remains at 600 rounds per minute, however.

The rifle can be used to launch conventional rifle grenades of Russian origin, including anti-tank and anti-personnel types. A 40mm grenade launcher, known as the Pallad, has been developed to allow an infantryman to fire these explosive projectiles out to ranges between 150m and 250m. A South African defence manufacturer has produced a 40mm grenade launcher known as the Mk 40, which is a single-shot, add-on device. This is compatible with various designs of assault rifle, including the AK47. The design of this launcher features a barrel that swings to the side for launching, which means it can accept the widest possible range of 40mm grenades, including smoke, illuminating and high explosive.

In summary, the AK47 is a no-frills weapon which even a conscript can use effectively after just a few lessons in basic weapons handling.

SPECIFICATIONS:

AK47

Calibre:	7.62mm x 39
Weight:	4.3kg
Length:	869mm with butt stock extended
	699mm with butt stock folded
Barrel:	414mm
Rifling:	Four grooves, right hand, one turn in 235mm
Muzzle velocity:	710m/sec

AKM

Calibre:	7.62mm x 39
Weight:	3.15kg
Length:	876mm overall
Barrel:	414mm
Rifling:	Four grooves, right hand, one turn in 235mm
Muzzle velocity:	715m/sec

The Russian-developed AK47 rifle with fixed wooden butt stock, and fitted with an LS45 laser sight. It is being trialled by a member of the British Army.

Member of the British Army evaluates the Russian AK47, with fixed wooden butt stock, and mounting an LS45 laser sight.

The standard calibre for the Russian Army during the Second World War was the 7.62mm x 39mm, and this was carried over into the post-war era known as the Cold War. However, following a trend in smaller calibres the Russians developed the AK74 rifle which fires a cartridge of 5.45mm x 39mm. It is essentially a reworked Kalashnikov AK47, with some minor but subtle differences. These include a change in muzzle brake design to reduce recoil and force the ejected gases sideways and upwards to reduce muzzle climb when the weapon is fired in fully automatic mode.

Another feature is that the bullet fired by the AK74 has a steel core with a boat-shaped tail. This projectile, which weighs 53 grains, has the unfortunate side-effect that it deforms and tumbles on striking the target. This can produce wounding effects which are worse than the normal type of bullet wound.

The AK74 has been developed into a series of weapons, including the RPK-74 which is similar to a Light Support Weapon, the AKS-74 with a folding butt stock, and the AKR-74 which is greatly reduced in length and intended to fulfil the role of a sub-machine gun. All these types were encountered at one time or another during the Russian involvement in Afghanistan between 1979 and 1988.

The AK74 uses the same receiver, stock, pistol grip and trigger mechanism as the AK47, which it closely resembles. The magazine for the AK74 contains 30 rounds and is manufactured from toughened plastic. The weapon fires at a cyclic rate of 650 rounds per minute. The magazine will also fit the magazine well of the AK47.

The Russian-designed and built AK-74 assault rifle as would have been used by the former East German Border Guards. Note brown-coloured butt stock which is manufactured from plastic and the 30-round box magazine, which is also plastic.

Re-created former East German Border Guard infantryman with an AK-74 assault rifle in 5.45mm calibre. Note the compact design of the rifle which comes from the same 'stable' as the more familiar AK-47. Note the brown-coloured plastic butt stock and magazine. This weapon is fitted with a sling which allows the man to carry it in his shoulder whilst performing other tasks.

The length of the round remains standard at 39mm, but the calibre of the AK74 is actually 2.17mm smaller than the 7.62mm round of the AK47. Some observers claim that the AK47 can fire this smaller round if necessary, but lack of proper gas obturation means there would be considerable falling off in range and accuracy.

The bolt of the AK74 is smaller than that fitted to the AK47, but the carrier and gas piston is the same between the weapons. The lighter bolt gives the weapon a better ratio of bolt to carrier mass, which in turn leads to improved functioning. The fire selector lever is still located on the right-hand side of the weapon and in the top, safe setting, serves the purpose of a dust cover, similar to the AK47. The rifle has a post-type front sight, protected by the usual tunnel-shaped protecting cover, and the rear sights are of the 'U' notch type.

Before the break-up of the Warsaw Pact the former

Detail of the breech of the Russian-designed AK-74 assault rifle. Note the fire selector switch and the rear sight which are made to withstand rough treatment in combat situations. The butt stock is fixed and manufactured from plastic. The 30-round magazine is also manufactured from brown plastic to reduce weight, without altering the weapon's cyclic rate of fire or ruggedness.

Soviet Union supplied quantities of the AK74 to satellite states. These were issued to most branches of the military, including Frontier Guards who would often fit knife-type bayonets. Russia and her former Warsaw Pact Allies have retained the AK74, despite the break-up of the Warsaw Pact and the establishment of the Confederation of Independent States, or CIS. The weapon has been well proven. For the same reason, any former client states in possession of the AK74 are unlikely to re-equip with anything else.

The AK74 has also been fitted with a 40mm grenade launcher, comparable in operation to the American M-203 as fitted to the M16. This allows an infantryman to engage targets such as light vehicles, as well as crew-served weapons like mortars, beyond the range at which he could throw a hand grenade. The AK74 was first seen fitted with this device in Afghanistan during the early 1980s at the time of the Russian invasion. The application of grenade launchers to assault rifles greatly increases the hitting power of an infantryman in close-quarter combat such as street fighting and house clearing.

SPECIFICATIONS:

Calibre:	5.45mm x 39
Weight:	3.6kg
Length:	930mm
	690mm (AKS-74 with butt stock folded)
Barrel:	400mm
Rifling:	Four grooves, right hand, one turn in 196mm
Muzzle velocity: 900m/sec	

The Spanish Army at present uses two versions of assault rifle, the Model L which has the straight lines of a conventional rifle with a fixed butt stock, and the Model LC, which is a shorter version of the design and has a retractable butt stock. Both versions fire the standard NATO 5.56mm x 45mm cartridge using a detachable box magazine with a 30-round capacity, and each weapon has a cyclic rate of 600 to 750 rounds per minute. The magazine is of the type used on the American M16 rifle.

The fire selector switch has settings marked 'T' for single shot and 'R' for automatic fire, as well as the usual 'Safe' setting. The safety setting works by locking up the trigger mechanism. The weapons are fitted with conical post front sights, which are protected, and flip-over rear sights which have only two settings, 200m and 400m.

Both weapons work on the delayed blowback principle, which also featured on earlier Spanish weapons. The weapons can be field stripped for cleaning and maintenance very easily by removing the two securing pins in the butt stock. This allows the butt stock itself to be removed, followed by the return spring and guide which are released from the body. The magazine must be removed prior to this operation to make sure the weapon is in an unloaded state and safe to handle. By pulling the cocking handle back, the bolt assembly can be removed through the rear of the receiver. The fire selector switch may also be removed and the hand grip is removed by withdrawing the pin and sliding it forward and downwards. The bolt assembly can be stripped for cleaning and the firing pin can also be stripped out if required. The weapon can be assembled and stripped without the need for tools.

The Model L weapon is also fitted with a bipod to the fore-end, which allows it to be supported when fired in the automatic mode from the prone position. In this manner it can be used as a Light Support Weapon, as with the British Army's LSW.

Spanish infantryman carrying the 'L' version assault rifle with a fixed butt stock.

SPECIFICATIONS:

(Model LC short assault rifle)

Calibre:	5.56mm x 45mm NATO
Weight:	3.40kg unloaded
Length:	925mm butt stock extended
	665mm butt stock retracted
Barrel:	400mm
Length of rifling:	320mm
Rifling:	Six grooves, right hand, one turn in 178mm
Muzzle velocity:	875m/sec

Although the SIG 540 range of assault rifles was designed and developed in Switzerland, they are manufactured only in Chile. They are all currently in service, in one form or another, with a number of countries including Bolivia, Chile, Gabon, Nigeria, Oman, Senegal and Swaziland.

All the designs in the range use gas operation with a rotating bolt The cocking handle is of the fixed-type which allows the firer to force the bolt closed if it becomes fouled, in the same way as other rifles with a fixed cocking handle design. The SG 540 and SG 543 both fire 5.56mm x 45 calibre rounds from box magazines of either 20- or 30-round capacity, and have cyclic rates of 650 to 800 rounds per minute. These two weapons are basically the same, the only significant difference being that the SG 543 has a shorter barrel which makes it 0.31kg lighter and 145mm shorter than the fixed butt stock version of the SG 540.

The SG 542 fires the 7.62mm x 51 round from a box magazine with either a 20- or 30-round capacity and, like the SG 540 and 543, has a cyclic rate of 650 to 800 rounds per minute. There is a special hold-open device which engages the follower of the magazine when the last round in that magazine has been fired. The firer inserts a new magazine into the magazine well, then releases the bolt by simply pulling the cocking handle slightly to the rear. This releases the bolt to move forward and chamber a new round, so firing can continue with the minimum of interruption.

All three of these SG assault rifle designs are available in either folding butt stock or fixed butt stock versions, and the 540 and 542 versions can be fitted with a folding bipod. This feature allows these weapons to serve as a light support weapon, when using a 30-round magazine. A bipod also allows them to be used as sniping rifles when equipped with a telescopic sights. The weapons can be fired in semi-automatic and fully automatic settings, with a three-round burst capability.

The weapon range functions perfectly well in all

Accessories for the SG 542 rifle, showing the folding butt stock of tubular design, the carrying sling, barrel cleaning brush and the socket-type bayonet. The optical sight unit is optional and can be fitted for use in place of the normal 'iron sights'.

(top) The SG 542 seen from the left-hand side. Note the bipod folded back along the length of the front stock, the magazine release catch in front of the trigger guard and the fire selector switch just above the pistol grip.

(bottom) The SG 542 rifle stripped down for cleaning, showing bolt assembly, return spring and piston rod and the hand guards of the front stock.

(middle) The SG 542 with folding butt stock seen from the right-hand side. Note the gas regulator above the barrel and the bipod which is folded back along the length of the front stock.

43

Opposite.

(top) The SG 542 with the bipod erected and the socket-type bayonet fitted, showing the classic lines of a modern assault rifle.

(upper middle) The SG 542 seen from the left-hand side. Note the sturdy construction of the fixed plastic butt stock and the grooves on the pistol grip to assist the firer in grasping the weapon firmly.

(lower middle) The SG 540 rifle stripped for cleaning. Similar in detail to the SG 542, it shows all the components which modern assault rifles feature, including rotating bolt assembly.

(bottom) The SG 540 seen from the right-hand side. It is fitted with a folding butt stock of tubular design and has a bipod folded back along the length of the front stock.

(top) The SG 540 seen from the right-hand side. It is fitted with a folding butt stock of tubular design and has a bipod folded back along the length of the front stock.

(middle) The SG 540 seen from the right-hand side. It is fitted with a fixed butt stock, 30-round magazine and bipod, seen here folded, to allow it to be used in the light support role.

(bottom) The SG 542 seen from the left-hand side. It is fitted with a standard 20-round magazine and features the fixed butt stock.

climates and terrain, and to allow firing in sub-zero conditions, when the firer would be wearing gloves or mittens, the trigger guard can be reversed. The trigger guard is also reversed when rifle grenades are fired from the muzzle of the weapon. When firing these munitions the gas regulator is set to 'zero' (fully closed) so that no gas passes into the cylinder – all the gas passes directly through the barrel to give more energy to launching the rifle grenade. The normal firing setting for the gas regulator is '1', with setting '2' reserved for tapping off more gas to cycle the weapon when fouling from sand, dust, water or debris is preventing the weapon from cycling normally.

The sights are identical on all three weapons in this range. The front sight is of the pillar type and is adjusted for zeroing by moving it up and down. The rear sight is a tilted drum which is rotated to the appropriate setting. The rear sights for the 5.56mm versions have increments from 100m to 500m whilst the 7.62mm SG 542 version has increments from 100m to 600m. The weapons can be fitted with a spike-type bayonet which has a tubular shaped handle to fit over the muzzle of the barrel. This means that the bullets are fired through the handle. It makes for a neat design, but results in the same problems as encountered on the British L85A1 rifle – after sustained firing the handle becomes too hot to hold, or even to remove the bayonet.

To field strip the weapons in this series the simple unloading procedure is first carried out. The magazine

View along the length of the SG 540 rifle, with bipod erected, to show the rear and front sights. Note the prominent cocking handle protruding from the right hand side of the weapon, midway down its length.

The SG 540 stripped for field cleaning, showing the main components including bolt assembly, gas cylinder and return spring, and receiver.

is removed and the bolt cocked to the rear to allow the chamber to be inspected and make sure the weapon is unloaded and safe to handle. The take-down pin, located above the pistol grip and slightly to the rear of the fire selector switch, is pressed out to allow the butt stock to be lowered along with the trigger group. The cocking handle is worked to the rear which moves the bolt back in the receiver. The cocking handle is then removed, and the whole bolt action can be withdrawn for cleaning. Further stripping involves removing the return spring and gas rod, along with the fore stock. The SG 540 breaks down into 12 components, counting the take-down pins, bolt assembly and cocking handle as individual items.

SPECIFICATIONS:

	SG 540	SG 542	SG 543
Calibre:	5.56mm	7.62mm	5.56mm
Weight:	3.26kg	3.55kg	2.95kg (with fixed butt stock)
	3.31kg	3.55kg	3.00kg (with folding butt stock)
Length:	950mm	1,000mm	805mm (with fixed butt stock)
	720mm	754mm	509mm (with folding butt stock)
Barrel:	460mm	465mm	300mm (without flash suppressor)
Rifling:	6 grooves	4 grooves	6 grooves
	1 turn in 305mm	1 turn in 305mm	1 turn in 305mm
Muzzle velocity:	980m/sec	820m/sec	875m/sec

The Swiss Industrial Company, SIG, developed the SG 550/551 series of rifles to meet specifications laid down by the Swiss Federal Army. The weapon was well received and accepted into service as the Sturmgewehr 90 assault rifle in 1984. Much use is made of plastic in the design, particularly in the forestock, butt stock, pistol grip and even the magazines. This has led to a dramatic saving in weight, without compromising the serviceability of the weapon.

Like its earlier counterparts, such as the SIG 540 and 550 series, the Sturmgewehr 90 has a three-round burst capability as well as single-shot and fully automatic. Firing a 5.56mm cartridge from either 20- or 30-round capacity magazines, the weapon has a cyclic rate of 700 rounds per minute. The series functions on a gas-operated cycle and uses a rotating bolt.

The SG 550 version is fitted with an integral bipod mounted on the fore-end, and using a 30-round magazine can function like a light support weapon. The SG 551 version is much shorter in length, and both versions have folding skeletal butt stocks. The weapons can be used to fire normal rifle grenades of all natures, including anti-tank and anti-personnel. The trigger guard can be reversed to allow the weapon to be used by the firer when he is wearing gloves or mittens in sub-zero conditions.

The SG 550/551 series features a hold-open device which operates after the last round of a magazine has been fired. When a new magazine is fitted the lock catch is activated and the firer can continue to use the weapon with the minimum amount of time spent in reloading. The transparent plastic magazines allow the firer to keep a visual check on the load status of the weapon. The magazines also feature studs and lugs on their sides which allow the firer to slot three magazines together, to eliminate the need to reach into an ammunition pouch

(left) **Swiss soldier wearing Simlas Torso Harness and carrying laser target pointer mounted on SIG Stgw 90 rifle SG 550. This system allows realistic training in the field.**

(below) **The SG 550 stripped down to show all the sub-assembly units, including the follower spring from the weapon's magazine. The bolt assembly has also been stripped down and the firing pin is visible between the legs of the bipod to the right of the picture. Note the knife-type bayonet and the well-equipped cleaning kit to the left of the picture.**

to retrieve a full magazine. This interlocking facility on magazines is much better than taping them together, because they can be separated easily for stowing.

The weapon series is fitted with a combined dioptre and alignment sight mounted on the breech, and this is fully adjustable in both windage and elevation. The alignment sight has luminous spots as an aiming aid in low light levels. When the daylight alignment sight is adjusted, the low light level sight is automatically adjusted at the same time. The front sight is protected

(top) **The SG 551 short version fitted with a telescopic sight unit and three magazines clipped together. Note the torch fitted underneath the barrel, which is for use when entering darkened rooms during house-clearing operations.**

(middle) **The short-barrelled SG 551 with folding butt stock.**

(bottom) **The long-barrelled SG 550 rifle fitted with a folding butt stock, seen from the right-hand side to show the ejector port and cocking handle.**

49

by a tunnel-shaped cover, and the rear sights are permanently fitted.

The SG 550/551 series can be fitted with image intensifier units to permit full use in night conditions. The mounting for this feature is standardised for the Swiss Army, but it is understood that a mounting which meets NATO STANAG 2324 can also be fitted. The rifles in this range can be fitted with knife-type bayonets for the assault stage of an infantry engagement.

For training purposes the SG 90 can be integrated with a Laser Target Pointer, with infantrymen wearing

(top) **The short-barrelled SG 551 fitted with telescopic sight. Note folding butt stock and well-shaped pistol grip.**

(bottom) **The short-barrelled SG 551 loaded with three transparent magazines clipped together for speed changing. The weapon is also fitted with a telescopic sight.**

the SIMLAS Torso Harness system. In this role the rifle is fitted to fire an eye-safe laser impulse at an infantryman wearing the receptor harness when a blank round is fired. These systems have been in use for a number of years

and they allow a level of battlefield training which borders on the realistic. A full magazine is loaded into the weapon and this will allow the firer to engage only those targets which have a coding to allow such engagements. For example, an infantryman can fire and register a 'kill' on another infantryman, but he cannot engage a main battle tank with his rifle. The chest harness which the infantryman wears for the purposes of these exercises mounts a number of sensors and another set for mounting on the helmet. These sensors detect a near miss, normally alerting the wearer with a short 'bleep'.

(top) **The SG 551 showing detail of the cocking handle and telescopic sight mounting unit.**

(middle) **The SG 550 showing the transparent magazine fitted into the magazine well and the folding butt stock extended.**

(bottom) **The SG 550 showing the butt stock folded forward.**

On receiving such an indication the wearer takes cover, as he would if he came under effective enemy fire for real. A direct hit is usually indicated by a continuous bleep **51** and this can only be turned off by an exercise umpire who is monitoring the whole scenario. These devices are now in quite widespread use and can be integrated into most rifle designs, including the G3, M16, sniping rifles and French FAMAS.

There is a commercial design of the SG 550/551 series which has the suffix letters 'SP' after the nomenclature, and fires only in the semi-automatic mode. In Switzerland, this version of the rifle is known as the Sturmgewehr 90 PE and is intended as a sporting weapon for target shooting. The inherent accuracy of

such a weapon means also that it would have a natural role in security or paramilitary forces where it could fulfil the role of a sniping rifle. This model of the SG 550/551

(top) **The SG 550 with a 40mm grenade launcher fitted under the front stock. Note the sights for the grenade are in the raised position by the rear sights. The grenade launcher has its own trigger mechanism for firing the projectile.**

(bottom) **Exploded diagram of the SG 550 assault rifle showing all the component parts.**

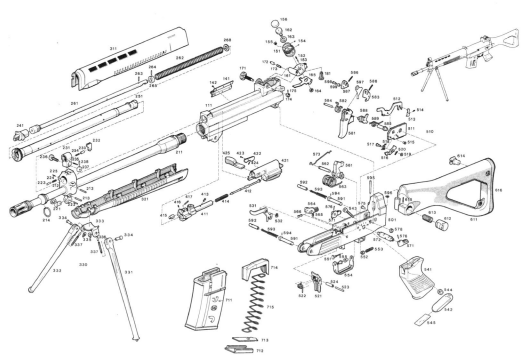

series is ballistically and dimensionally identical to the military version except that it cannot fire in the fully automatic mode.

The SG 550 can be fitted with a 40mm grenade launcher of SIG manufacture. This is an add-on feature and functions in a similar manner to other 40mm grenade launchers, with its own trigger mechanism, and is capable of firing a wide range of ammunition types.

SPECIFICATIONS:

	SG 550	SG 551
	Standard version	Short version
Calibre:	5.56mm x 45	5.56mm x 45
Weight:	4.1kg	3.5kg (unloaded, with bipod)
Length:	998mm	827mm (butt stock extended)
	772mm	601mm (butt stock folded)
Barrel:	528mm	372mm
Rifling:	Six grooves	Six grooves
	Right hand	Right hand

(top left) **British infantryman carrying the L85A1 rifle, also known as the SA80.**

(bottom left) **British infantryman holding the L85A1 rifle. Note the SUSAT sight unit which is used more commonly than the weapon's iron sights.**

(above) **British infantryman taking up the aim using the SUSAT sight fitted to the L85A1 rifle. Note the short length and low profile of the weapon.**

Until the early 1980s the British Army used the venerable L1A1 SLR which was originally designed by Fabrique Nationale of Herstal in Belgium. This rifle fired 7.62mm calibre rounds and had served the British Army through many conflicts, from Aden, Northern Ireland and the Falkland Islands.

In 1987 the British Army was issued with the first units of a new rifle design, which today is known as the L85A1 rifle. The L85A1 is currently in service with the Royal Marines as well as all branches of the British Army, including the Parachute Regiment. The rifle fires the 5.56mm calibre round and is of the bullpup layout. Unlike certain other, similar designs, the L85A1 did not have a smooth transition from experimentation into service issue. During its development trials the rifle was known as the XL70 E3 (Individual Weapon), and was originally designed to fire a round of 4.85mm calibre. There is not much one can say about this rifle that is not already known, and the number of negative reports are almost as legendary as the number of changes made to the weapon's basic design layout.

When the L85A1 first emerged it bore an uncanny

British infantryman takes aim in the kneeling position with the L85A1. He is aiming through the SUSAT sight unit which provides excellent target acquisition.

resemblance to the EM2 rifle of 1952 vintage, which fired a 7mm cartridge. The new rifle was for a time referred to as the 'SA80', before being given the reference L85A1, and it is still often known by the shorter term of SA80. The transition for the British Army moving from the L1A1 self-loading rifle, SLR, to the L85A1 was not a simple move. Due to a shortage of supply of the new rifle, the changeover did not happen in one simple process, as should have should have been the case. Difficulties in manufacturing delayed production, which in turn caused further changeover problems. The change in calibre from 4.85mm to allow the weapon to fire the new NATO standard round of 5.56mm calibre also created its own set of problems.

The L85A1 is the rifle version of a series of weapons in a range which includes a version for use by young cadets, who have to cock the weapon after every shot. The Light Support Weapon in the range has a longer barrel than the L85A1, and is fitted with a bipod to allow it to be used as a light machine gun. The two weapons have a high degree of commonality of parts, including magazines and bolt carrier.

The rifle uses box magazines of 30-round capacity and has a cyclic rate of 650 to 800 rounds per minute, which is comparable to other bullpup design rifles. The trigger has a pull weight set between 3.12kg and 4.5kg. A distinguishing feature on the L85A1 rifle is its large carrying handle, comparable to that fitted to the M16, which incorporates the rear sights of the 'iron sights' with the front sight mounted on a removable post protected by blades. The carrying handle can also be removed to allow the fitting of a SUSAT sight with x4 magnification for normal battlefield use. The same mounting bracket, which has a dovetail base, also allows a range of night-vision equipment to be fitted to the L85A1. The rifle has an effective range up to 400m, which is the optimum

British infantryman prepares to use the L85A1 left handed, despite the fact that it cannot be configured to such a role for the safety and comfort of the firer. The FAMAS and AUG, the other two bullpup designs in service, can be configured for left-handed firers.

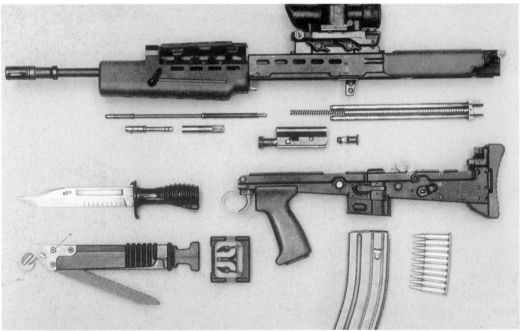

(top) British infantryman with L85A1 rifle showing detail of the SUSAT sight unit.

(bottom) The British Army's L85A1 rifle stripped down to show its rather complicated mechanism. Note the knife-type bayonet which can also be used with the scabbard as a wirecutter.

Opposite.

(top) British troops inside the EH 101 troop-carrying helicopter. The compact design of the L85A1 makes it suitable for troops deploying from such confined environments as helicopters and APCs.

(bottom) The British Royal Marines also use the L85A1 rifle. It is seen here fitted with SUSAT sights as standard.

engagement distance for infantrymen on the battlefield.

The rifle is manufactured from stamped and machined parts and plastic material for the pistol grip, forestock and butt plate. The L85A1 is fitted with a carrying sling which is fully adjustable and allows the carrier to place it in a position which allows him to perform tasks with his hands without putting the weapon down. This is similar in practice to the French Army's FAMAS rifle.

The rifle can fire rifle grenades of all natures, but trials into mounting a 40mm grenade launcher were curtailed early on in the development programme. This particular device fired standard 40mm grenades out to a maximum range of 350m and featured all the usual safety mechanisms, with automatic opening and ejection. Unfortunately the launcher added 1.4kg to the weight of the rifle, which was an unacceptable burden, and it never entered service on the L85A1 rifle. A much shortened version of the rifle with a snub-barrel was proposed and trialled to initial development phases. But after some initial interest, that programme, too, was cut short.

The rifle features the familiar gas-operated type of mechanism locked by a rotating bolt which engages in lugs behind the breech and is carried on two guide rods. The cocking handle is on the right-hand side of the weapon. On operating this to load the weapon the ejection port cover – which also acts as a 'dust cover' – is opened. Unlike the Austrian-designed AUG rifle of bullpup layout, the L85A1 cannot be configured to suit left-handed firers. The rifle can be fitted with a blank firing attachment for training in field exercises. A knife-type bayonet can be fitted, but this too has come in for criticism. The design uses a hollow handle, which means it fits completely around the muzzle of the weapon rather than using an adapter ring and mounting lug under the barrel. This means that when the rifle is fired with the bayonet fitted the bullets and hot gases pass through the handle and heat it up. This makes it virtually impossible to remove the bayonet after firing without gloves.

The L85A1 is used by units of the British Army deployed to the Province of Northern Ireland. The weapon was also used by British troops committed to the Coalition forces during Operation DESERT STORM against Iraq in 1990–91, and more recently is used by troops deployed with UN forces conducting peacekeeping missions in areas such as Bosnia.

Overall the weapon appears to function well, but

A member of the British Royal Marines takes aim with his L85A1 rifle using the SUSAT sight.

compared to other bullpup designs, especially the AUG, it is not faultless. The author has fired the L85A1 a number of times and whilst it is comfortable and the SUSAT allows for good target acquisition, he never felt entirely at ease with the weapon. Unofficial reports have filtered out suggesting that troops serving with the Coalition forces during Operation DESERT STORM were far from satisfied with the operational capabilities of the L85A1. Even if one dismisses 90 per cent of these reports as simple moaning, there is still some cause for concern.

The rifle appears to perform well in the temperate climates encountered in Northern Ireland and central Europe, but in more extreme climates it clearly has difficulties. This helps to explain its lack of export success. The Austrian bullpup design, the AUG, has been sold extensively, and even the French FAMAS has been taken in small numbers, although not to the extent of re-equipping entire overseas armed forces. The L85A1, on the other hand, has yet to attract even remote interest from potential overseas clients. Given the continuing adverse reports of the rifle, it looks unlikely that this position will change in the future. The production run of the L85A1 rifle for the British Army is now complete, with over 300,000 units having been built.

SPECIFICATIONS:

Calibre:	5.56mm x 45
Weight:	3.9kg (unloaded and without SUSAT sight)
Weight:	5.04kg (with 30-round magazine and SUSAT sight fitted)
Length:	770mm
Barrel:	518mm
Rifling:	Six grooves, right hand, one turn in 180mm
Muzzle velocity:	900m/sec

There is not much one can say that is new about the US Army's 5.56mm x 45mm M16 rifle. Along with the Russian AK47, the M16 stands as one of the most instantly recognisable rifles of modern times, and has been accepted into service by numerous armies around the world, including Australia, Canada, New Zealand, Israel – even some elements of the British Army have used it.

Since its appearance back in the early 1960s the M16 has influenced many designs of weapon, and has

(top) **M16A2 fitted with the Rifleman's Assault Weapon, RAW, which has a HESH effect on the target. The launching device clips to the muzzle of the rifle and requires no special launching ammunition. Unusually, the M16A2 seen here is fitted with a bipod.**

(bottom) **An American serviceman takes aim with his M16A2 rifle using the RAW HESH system. Note he takes direct aim and the device for launching the RAW is simply clipped to the muzzle of the weapon.**

(above) **An American airborne infantryman takes up firing position with his M16A2 fitted with an M203 40mm grenade launcher.**

(left) **An American airborne infantryman has just landed and is stowing his equipment. He has his M16A2 rifle ready to hand.**

M16A2. Often referred to as 'The Black Rifle' the M16 is a popular service rifle and has been used in countless military engagements around the world from temperate zones to extremes of desert heat and Arctic conditions and still functioned reliably.

The origins of the M16 are as well known as those of the Galil or AK47, but, to recap briefly, the rifle was designed by Eugene Stoner and originally appeared in the early 1960s as the AR-15, with the intention of firing the newly-developed 5.56mm calibre round. Successful trials led to it being adapted and taken into service use by the US Army, which at the time was heavily engaged in the Vietnam War in South East Asia. The rifle was given the service title of M16. The US Air Force quickly followed the lead of the Army and adopted the rifle too, and today there are few American Government agencies which do not have their own stock or access to a stock of M16 rifles, including police forces, FBI, Coast Guard and the Drug Enforcement Agency.

However good any weapon may be, there is always room for improvement, and combat experience in Vietnam showed that some alterations had to be made.

even been copied directly by the Chinese. This last version was termed 'CQ' by the Chinese, which means '16', and was a copy of the M16A1 version of the rifle. It differed from the original only by having a curved pistol grip with some embellishments. If imitation is the sincerest form of flattery, then this was high praise indeed. The M16 has appeared in many authorised versions and been the subject of much experimentation.

The standard version in current service today is the

(top) **A member of the British TA using an M16A1 on an exercise. The British Army has used the M16 for many years and it is regarded as a useful weapon and is very popular with those troops who have used it.**

(bottom) **The American-built M16A2 seen here being trialled by a British serviceman using the LS45 laser sight device. The M16 is capable of being used to mount a great variety of optical sights.**

(right) **Two Guardsmen, of the 1st Battalion Irish Guards of the British Army, patrol the troubled streets of Aden during the crisis in 1966. They are carrying M16A1s, at around the same time that American troops were beginning to receive them for operational use in the Vietnam War.**

The most obvious one was the call for a bolt return plunger, today referred to as 'forward assist', which would allow an infantryman to close the bolt of the weapon if it became jammed through fouling as the result of continued use in combat.

The current M16A2 rifle fires the SS109 round from a detachable box magazine with a 30-round capacity, and has a cyclic rate between 700 and 950 rounds per minute. The effective range of the M16A2 is set at 400m, which is nowadays seen as the optimum engagement range for infantry small arms fire. The different versions of the M16, which have appeared at various times, have included a 'firing port' model for use from inside a Mechanised Infantry Combat Vehicle, or MICV, and the Colt 'Commando' with a collapsible butt stock and shortened barrel. There have also been trials to develop a heavy-barrelled version fitted with a bipod to serve in the role of a squad light support weapon.

The M16 has been used by US service personnel in many engagements, including Grenada in 1983, UN peacekeeping roles around the world, and during Operation DESERT STORM in the Gulf War of 1990–91, against Iraqi forces which had invaded Kuwait.

The M16 can be fitted with a knife-type bayonet and blank firing muzzle attachments for training purposes. The standard M16A2 has a fixed butt stock, manufactured from plastic, the same as the forestock. The flash illuminator is of the type known as a 'birdcage' and the distinctive carrying handle, which also

incorporates the rear sights, has been retained.

The M203 40mm grenade launcher was developed to be fitted to the M16. The original design was a rather bulky, heavy affair but it has been refined over the years and greatly reduced in weight. This device can fire all natures of 40mm grenades including high explosive, anti-tank, anti-personnel, smoke and illuminating. Another 'force multiplying' weapon developed for the M16 rifle was the High Explosive Squash Head – Rifleman's Assault Weapon (HESH-RAW). Developed by the American company of Brunswick Defense, it is seen as a projectile for use in military operations in urban areas (MOUA), or fighting in built-up areas (FIBUA), as it is described in British military terminology. HESH-RAW is a rocket-propelled munition launched from the muzzle of an M16 rifle using a special adapter. The adapter fits easily to the rifle, and the projectile is launched by the firer using his weapon in the direct firing mode from the shoulder. Because it is a line of sight weapon it is aimed at the target using the rifle's ordinary sights. The HESH-RAW projectile is spherical in shape and weighs some 8.5lb with an explosive payload of some 2.5lb. It can be used to destroy light vehicles as well as machine-gun emplacements, mortar sites, and other strengthened positions. It has no backblast, which means an infantyman can use it from the confines of a building – a useful feature in FIBUA operations. In the direct fire mode the infantryman can engage targets out to 200m, and in the indirect fire mode the HESH-RAW will carry out to **63**

2,000m. Although effective, HESH-RAW is a rather bulky munition and if a serviceman were to be given the option between this and several rounds of 40mm grenades for his M203 launcher, he would refuse the HESH-RAW.

The M16 is easy to come to terms with and handling during firing is comfortable, even during the three-round burst sequence. Field stripping for cleaning and maintenance is simple and quick. The take-down pin on the left of the rear of the receiver is pushed through and the butt stock and lower receiver swung down. The bolt carrier assembly and cocking handle can then be slid out and separated. The hand guard is removed, and the buffer and return spring can then be extracted. To reassemble the rifle the stripping sequence is reversed. It takes only a few minutes to achieve and the rifle will function perfectly even under the most arduous of conditions.

SPECIFICATIONS:

Calibre:	5.56mm x 45mm
Length:	990mm overall
Weight:	3.18kg
Barrel:	508mm
Rifling:	Six grooves, right hand, one turn in 305mm
Muzzle velocity:	1000m/sec

SNIPING RIFLES

Sniping rifles, like shotguns, have a broad band of users, ranging from police in urban situations to paramilitary forces and the regular military who use snipers on the battlefield for harassment and disruption of the enemy.

The terrorist gunman, erroneously called a sniper, using a semi-automatic weapon, should not be confused with the shooter who has spent many long hours honing his skill to a standard which is second to none.

Historically snipers were excellent shots equipped with well-made rifles fitted with telescopic sights and supplied with special ammunition to engage targets at extreme ranges, well beyond the normal limits of engagement for infantrymen with ordinary rifles. During the American Civil War, for example, sharp-shooters in the Army of the Confederate States used Whitworth rifles of .450 inch calibre with a hexagonal bore to snipe at Federal troops on the battlefield. The Union Generals Sedgewick and Lytle are believed to have been casualties of such sniping tactics with these rifles.

Sniping in the First World War was much in evidence on both sides of the Western Front Theatre, and by 1918 the British Army was issuing Mk.1* W(T) .303 inch calibre Lee-Enfield rifles at the rate of three per battalion. These weapons were solely for the purpose of sniping and not for an ordinary rifleman's trench warfare. Sniping continued throughout the Second World War and the Russian Army even resorted to using women in the role of battlefield snipers, equipped with the bolt action 7.62mm calibre Mosin-Nagant M1891/30 fitted with a telescopic sight.

The British Army's thinking on the psychology of a sniper at the time was that he should be: '...of above average intelligence, strong, and tireless, have the makings of a good shot, have a liking for being alone and should, for preference, be a countryman'. The fact that this definition of a potential sniper demands only that he should 'have the makings' of a good shot, and not necessarily be an excellent shot indicates that a man can be properly coached in the art of sniping. As a trained sniper at the British Army's Infantry School for Small Arms at Warminster informed the author, the actual

taking of the shot is the 'cherry on the cake'. The rest of the engagement, such as the waiting time and the sighting, is equally important. On the battlefield the sniper is a lone wolf. His actions are one-on-one, making sniping one of the most personal of all types of engagement.

In post-war years the requirements for snipers and sniping fell off in most armies, and as a battlefield role it was destined not to regain its former importance until the Korean War. During that conflict both sides employed snipers to good effect, and some individuals made an impressive tally of kills. The British Army was one of the first forces to realise the error of its ways in allowing sniping to deteriorate, and set about remedying its deficiency in battlefield snipers.

The sniper's skills of fieldcraft and marksmanship are as important as his rifle, but naturally snipers are armed with well-made, accurate rifles – usually with a bolt action, fitted with high quality telescopic sights and firing matched ammunition. The sniper's rifle has all manner of features which allow him to 'tailor' it to suit his specific build, including adjustable cheek-plates on the butt-stock, adjustable butt plates, bipods and balancing weights.

The preferred rifle type for police or military snipers for engaging specific, high priority targets, sometimes presenting themselves in an opportune manner, is the bolt action type. There are a handful of very well-designed semi-automatic types which deliver good results. But it must be said that for precise, accurate shooting, rather than volume of fire, the bolt action designs are without equal.

The primary role of the modern military sniper is to create an air of uncertainty in all areas of the battlefield, from the front line to areas extending some several hundred metres to the rear. Troops can never afford to relax their guard if they are aware that snipers are present in the vicinity. A sniper may be anything up to 1,000 metres from the enemy's front line, and he must be able to engage and hit a human-sized target with great precision at this range.

The sniper's skills of concealment and observation also make him a vital ingredient of an army's intelligence-gathering system. With suitable communications, he can report important details of the enemy's strength and movements. The sniper also plays this crucial role in hostage situations involving police or military anti-terrorist forces.

To aid the sniper in his task he is equipped with the finest optical equipment including, for night time, either thermal imaging or passive infra-red sights, to enable him to engage targets 24 hours a day. But even the finest tools will fail if the man is not up to the task, and ultimately the sniper has to rely on his skill, judgment and patience to engage a target successfully.

The TRG sniping rifle from the Finnish company of Sako is available in two models, which share a high degree of commonality in parts, with only the calibres and length of rifling varying between the two models. The TRG rifle has been developed through a highly detailed study of a sniper's requirements. The resulting weapon is one which is primarily for military use and has an accuracy that delivers half a minute of angle. At ranges of 1,000m the rifle in a well trained sniper's hands is capable of consistently placing rounds in a target of some 100mm diameter.

The TRG is a robustly designed weapon, and has substantial weight to match its overall dimensions. The action body of the TRG rifle is triangular in section, with the bottom of the body being flat and the sides angled inwards with flat outer surfaces and rounded inner guides for the bolt. The action is bedded onto an aluminium alloy bedding block. The barrel length of the TRG-21 is

660mm and on the TRG-41 it is 690mm in length. In both cases the barrels are manufactured from cold hammer-forged metal and are free-floating, with some 6.5mm clearance from the bedding block.

The muzzle brake is threaded to permit a suppressor to be fitted if tactical requirements demand it. In this case special subsonic ammunition would be used, such as the 7.62mm x 51 which is full metal jacket with a velocity in the order of 315 metres per second. The projectile of this round weighs 12g and the tip is painted

(top) **The Finnish TRG sniping rifle stripped down to its component parts showing the trigger mechanism, barrel and bolt assembly.**

(bottom) **The Finnish TRG sniping rifle without any added features such as telescopic sight. Note its very plain, almost simple, lines.**

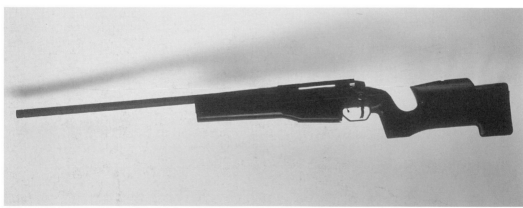

blue for ease of identification. This ammunition demands a barrel with a maximum 435mm twist.

The trigger mechanism is detachable and has a double stage pull. The first take-up pressure can be set at 1kg and the second to 2.5kg, and the trigger can also be adjusted for length of pull and vertical or horizontal pitch. The bolt of the TRG rifle has three forward locking lugs, and the firing pin has a travelling distance of 6.5mm before striking the round. The bolt lift angle in both versions of the TRG is 60 degrees, but the TRG-21 has a bolt throw of 98mm, whilst the TRG-41 has a bolt throw of 118mm. The handle on the bolt is an over-large knob to allow the firer ease of action even in the coldest of conditions. For the best possible stability and rigidity, the aluminium base stock of the rifle is fitted with a polyurethane forestock. The butt stock, also manufactured from polyurethane, has an aluminium skeleton.

The rifle is equipped with a folding bipod and the cheekpiece can be adjusted for height, windage and pitch. The butt plate is also fully adjustable and can be altered to suit individual shooter's requirements in length and horizontal or vertical pitch. The TRG rifle designs have detachable box magazines, which on the TRG-21 model has a capacity of 10 rounds and on the TRG-41 five rounds. The rifles are not supplied with optical sights but the mounting rail will accept most types of sighting units, including night-vision equipment with STANAG 2324.

(right) **Close-up detail showing the massive action body of the TRG sniping rifle, which is triangular in shape.**

(below) **The Finnish TRG sniping rifle fitted with both telescopic sight and night-vision device. Note the muzzle brake fitted to the muzzle to give the firer better control of the weapon.**

SPECIFICATIONS

	TRG-21	TRG-41
Calibre:	.308 Win. (7.62mm)	.338 Lapua Mag. (8.58mm)
Overall length:	1,150mm	1,200mm
		(without butt spacers)
Weight:	4.7kg	5.1kg
Barrel length:	660mm	690mm
Muzzle velocity:	760m/sec with 7.62mm x 51 full metal jacket	
Rifling:	Four grooves,	Four grooves,
	right hand, one	right hand, one
	turn in 435mm	turn in 305mm

The French-designed and -built Fusil à Répétition Modèle F1, or FR-F1 sniping rifle, has been declared obsolete in use with the French Army, but like other weapons which have been sold to many users it is still likely to be encountered in many theatres of operation around the world.

This particular rifle can be supplied in either 7.5mm x 54, a round much used by the French before the advent of the 5.56mm, or the 7.62mm x 51, which is NATO standard. To differentiate between the calibres, and avoid costly mistakes, the calibre of the weapon is stamped on the left-hand side of the receiver.

The FR-F1 was designed to replace the ageing Modèle 1936, which was also in 7.5mm calibre, and provided the French Army with a reliable and accurate weapon. The FR-F1 is a bolt-action rifle with a ten-round detachable box magazine, capable of firing out to ranges of 800m at a rate of 10–15 rounds per minute. However, a sniper would seldom be expected to fire that many rounds in the course of one minute, and more selective firing would achieve better results. No left-handed version of the rifle was made, and all models were equipped with basic iron sights.

The locking lugs on the bolt are rear-mounted and on operating the action after firing a cam bears against the surface at the rear of the receiver and full movement of the bolt performs extraction of the spent case, in an action common to many bolt-action rifles. Pushing the bolt forward strips a round from the magazine and feeds it into the chamber, and the locking action of the bolt forces the extractor grips around the rim of the cartridge in readiness to extract the round after firing. At the same time, the sear holds up the firing pin lug to retain the firing pin in the cocked position.

The trigger has the usual two-stage pressure associated with sniping rifles. When the firer takes up the first pressure, the trigger bears on the trigger pin, joining the trigger and sear until the trigger stud reaches the bottom of the receiver. The second take-up pressure pivots the sear and compresses the spring, until the sear releases the lug of the firing pin which moves forward to strike the base of the round.

The FR-F1 is fitted with a bipod which has fully adjustable legs attached to the body of the rifle mid-way along its length to give a good point of balance. The butt

The French FR-F1 sniping rifle has been replaced by the FR-F2, but may still be found in use by various forces around the world. Note the bipod placed at a good point of balance and the adjustable cheek-plate on the butt stock.

stock has fully adjustable butt-plate spacers and cheek-plate. The forestock, butt and pistol grip are all manufactured from wood.

The FR-F1 can accept a wide range of optical sights, including night-vision equipment, but the x4 Modèle 53 telescopic sight is preferred. The magazine of the rifle has a rubber top cover which is removed before inserting into the magazine well and there is the facility to top up the magazine one round at a time, should the sniper feel it necessary.

Snipers of the 2nd Parachute Battalion of the French Foreign Legion (2e Bataillon Etranger Parachutiste; 2 BEP) were equipped with the FR-F1 when they were successfully deployed to the Shaba province in southern Zaire in May 1978. The fighting to restore order to this former Belgian colony was intense, and during this relatively short operation sniping was much in evidence. In fact, one of the first French casualties during the deployment, Corporal Arnold, fell to sniper fire.

SPECIFICATIONS:

Calibre:	7.5mm x 54 or 7.62mm x 51
Weight (empty):	5.2kg
Overall length:	1,138mm (without butt spacers)
Barrel length:	552mm
Rifling:	Four grooves, right hand, one turn in 305mm
Muzzle velocity:	Around 852m/sec, depending on type of ammunition

Just as the FR-F1 sniping rifle was introduced to replace the Modèle 1936, so the Fusil à Répétition Modèle F2, or FR-F2, has been introduced as a modern replacement for the FR-F1. The FR-F2 fires the NATO 7.62mm x 51 calibre, with which it has a firing stoppage rate better than 10^3. The FR-F2 is a bolt-action rifle and its most obvious difference from the earlier FR-F1 is the heavier barrol which is fitted with a flash suppressor, protected by a monobloc stock, and is bolted to the breech casing. The life of the barrel is claimed to be better than 12,000 rounds with no loss of accuracy, and some 20,000 rounds with accuracy remaining better than 90 per cent of the original value.

The breech casing also supports the butt stock and has guide rails on its upper surfaces to accept the mounting for the telescopic sight. The FR-F2 can be supplied in either the wooden monobloc stock design or with a composite material stock. The former serves to protect the barrel and support the integral bipod. The composite material design allows the barrel to be fitted using heat-shrink processes and a ball-jointed bipod to be mounted which makes the tracking of moving targets much easier.

The trigger mechanism comprises the cam action trigger, the sear, and its spring. The cams are fully adjustable and the pull force of the trigger can be set in the order of 2 daN. The safety catch is located to the left of the trigger guard and when applied locks up the trigger action.

The butt stock features an adjustable cheek plate, and insert plates can be fitted or removed to adjust the length to suit individual users. The rifle can accept most optical units and the scope mounting has a simple-to-use cam-type locking lever for quick fitting and removal. A typical daytime telescopic sight of 6 x 42 magnification will allow accurate target engagements out to 800m. For night use the FR-F2 can be fitted with a light-intensified device such as the SOPELEM OB50, which has a x 3 magnification and a ten degree field of view. This night-vision device will allow a sniper to engage targets out to 150m with a light level at 10^3 lux and 400m at 10^1 lux.

The box magazine is identical to the type fitted to the older FR-F1 sniping rifle. It holds ten rounds and can be reloaded one round at a time if required.

The FR-F2 can be used in temperatures ranging from -40°C to +51°C, which makes it versatile enough to equip troops operating in all types of terrain from desert to Arctic warfare.

The French Army's FR-F2 sniping rifle which has replaced the older FR-F1. Here a sniper is seen taking aim showing the rifle's bipod and heavy barrel.

SPECIFICATIONS:

Calibre: 7.62mm x 51

Overall length: 1,200mm

Length of barrel: 650mm.

Weight: 4.45kg (with wooden stock)

5.34kg (with wooden stock and telescopic sight)

4.84kg (with composite stock)

5.74kg (with composite stock and telescopic sight)

Length of rifling: 582mm

Rifling: Three grooves, right hand, one turn in 295mm

The French Army's FR-F2 sniping rifle standing on its bipod. It is fitted with a telescopic sight. Note the flash eliminator on the muzzle.

The G3 SG/1 sniping rifle from the design team of the German company of Heckler and Koch is essentially a modified version of the standard G3A3 semi-automatic rifle. The Scharfschützen Gewehr, SG/1, was developed for the German police, who use the weapon with either a telescopic sight or the weapon's integral iron sights.

The sniping version is not manufactured on a dedicated sniping rifle production line but is the result of standard rifles demonstrating their ability consistently to place their mean point of impact correctly during proof firing trials. Those weapons which meet the high standard required for precision marksmanship are set aside for modification into sniping versions.

Those weapons which qualify for modification are fitted with a special trigger group which incorporates a 'set' trigger with a variable pull. In the 'set' position, the trigger requires only the slightest touch to fire the round. The trigger can only be 'set' when the combined fire selector switch/safety catch is set to the 'E' position, for 'single shots'. The trigger can be reset after firing one round, or the firer can continue to use the weapon without making any adjustment to the trigger which has a full take-up pull in the order of 2.6kg. If the trigger has been 'set' this is automatically released as soon as the fire selector switch is moved from 'single shot' to 'safe' or 'automatic'. However, it is unlikely that a sniper would ever use the latter mode of fire, as single shot is more in keeping with the traditional sniping role.

The G3 SG/1 fires the standard 7.62mm x 51 round and is fitted with a 20-round magazine. It cycles in exactly the same way as the standard G3 rifle, which is based on delayed blowback. This makes it readily familiar to many police and service personnel. Iron sights are fitted as standard on this sniping rifle but an optical sight unit such as a Zeiss variable power 1.5-6x can be clamped to a side rail running along the left-hand side of the receiver for use in the true sniping role. This combination has full windage and range adjustments to ranges between 100m and 600m, which is probably the full

Cut-away diagram showing the trigger mechanism of the G3 SG/1 German sniping rifle.

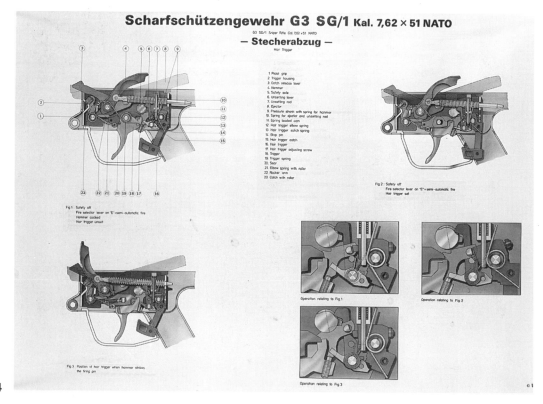

Scharfschützengewehr G3 SG/1 Kal. 7,62 × 51 NATO

G3 SG/1 Sniper Rifle Cal.7,62 ×51 NATO

— Stecherabzug —

Hair Trigger

1 Pistol grip
2 Trigger housing
3 Catch release lever
4 Hammer
5 Safety axle
6 Unsetting lever
7 Unsetting rod
8 Ejector
9 Pressure shank with spring for hammer
10 Spring for ejector and unsetting rod
11 Spring loaded cam
12 Hair trigger elbow spring
13 Hair trigger catch spring
14 Stop pin
15 Hair trigger catch
16 Hair trigger
17 Hair trigger adjusting screw
18 Trigger
19 Trigger spring
20 Sear
21 Elbow spring with roller
22 Rocker arm
23 Catch with roller

Fig 1. Safety off
Fire selector lever on 'E'-semi-automatic fire
Hammer cocked
Hair trigger unset

Fig 2. Safety off
Fire selector lever on 'E'-semi-automatic fire
Hair trigger set

Fig 3. Position of hair trigger when hammer strikes the firing pin

Operation relating to Fig.1

Operation relating to Fig 2

Operation relating to Fig 3

engagement range that police snipers will encounter in urban situations.

The G3 SG/1 sniping rifle has an adjustable bipod fitted to the front end of the forestock and the barrel is equipped with a flash suppressor, as on the standard G3 rifle design. The butt-stock of the SG/1 has an adjustable cheek-plate, and its length can be altered by

(left) **A police sniper takes aim using the G3 SG/1 rifle. He is using the telescopic UA1126 night sight to show the configuration during daylight conditions. Due to his unconventional firing position he has folded the bipod legs back along the length of the forestock.**

(top) **The G3 SG/1 sniping rifle seen from the left-hand side showing the mounting bracket for the standard telescopic sight. Note the adjustable bipod and the cocking handle in the usual position as featured on the normal G3 assault rifle.**

(below) **Exploded diagram of the G3 SG/1 sniping rifle showing all the components, including trigger mechanism and bolt assembly.**

inserting spacers to the butt-plate.

As well as the German police, the SG/1 is in use with several other police forces including the Italian Carabinieri. It should be pointed out, however, that the SG/1 is not the first version of the G3 rifle to be fitted with a telescopic sight. The G3A3Z ('Z' being zielfernrohr for telescope) was an early experimental version, but did not enter general service.

(top) **The G3 SG/1 German semi-automatic sniping rifle seen from the left-hand side with the bipod legs folded and fitted with telescopic sight.**

(bottom) **The G3 SG/1 semi-automatic sniping rifle seen from the left-hand side with bipod erected.**

SPECIFICATIONS:

Calibre:	7.62mm x 51
Overall length:	1,016mm (without spacers)
Weight unloaded:	4.25kg
Barrel length:	450mm
Rifling:	Four grooves, right hand
Muzzle velocity:	Typically in the order of 805m/sec

The Präzisionsschützengewehr (High Precision Marksman's Rifle), or PSG 1, has been developed by Heckler and Koch in response to demands by police and military snipers for high precision weapons. It is one of a handful of semi-automatic rifles to be used in the sniping role, but is limited to delayed blowback, single-fire operation.

As may be imagined, the PSG 1 is a heavy weapon, but the integral bipod and adjustable pistol grip rest plate mean that the firer does not have to support the weight for prolonged periods. The rifle utilises the standard breech mechanism, whereby the bolt is a two-part unit with delayed opening which is achieved through the roller-locked system. The weapon's cycle of operation is familiar to many service personnel. The bolt system, however, has been modified so that when cycling and closing it has a much reduced signature.

The trigger has also been altered so that it has the sniper's favoured two-stage take-up pressure. Adjustments are made by means of a vertically adjustable trigger-shoe to provide variable-width trigger with a take-up pressure of some 1.5kg. The butt stock has fully adjustable cheek-plates and butt-plate to suit the individual anatomy of the shooter.

The PSG 1 fires 7.62mm NATO rounds and is fed by means of a box magazine, which is available in either 5-round or 20-round capacity. Used by an experienced sniper, this weapon is capable of placing ten rounds inside a target area 50mm square at 300m range. The PSG 1 will accept most types of optical sights, including night-vision units. It is normally fitted with a 6 x 42 telescopic sight, which is unusual in that adjustments for windage and elevation are made by movement of

(top) **The semi-automatic PSG 1 sniping rifle showing adjustable plate, cheek-plate and hand grip.**

(bottom) **The semi-automatic PSG 1 sniping rifle stripped for cleaning. Visible are the various components, including trigger assembly, bolt assembly and return spring.**

The German semi-automatic PSG 1 sniping rifle seen here from the left-hand side with telescopic sight fitted and bipod

the internal optical system. There are six settings to allow for ranges between 100m and 600m, and there is also a fine adjustment facility to compensate for any mounting offset angle.

SPECIFICATIONS:

Calibre:	7.62mm x 51 NATO. Also Lapua .308 Winchester Match Ammunition
Weight:	7.2kg
Overall length:	1,208mm
Barrel length:	650mm
Rifling:	Four grooves, right hand
Magazine capacity:	5 or 20 rounds

The Galil assault rifle as used by the Israeli Defence Forces is available in both 5.56mm and 7.62mm calibres, and has been combat proven many times during which the design has stood up well to the rigours of the battlefield. It was only a natural progression that a sniping version of the Galil should be developed, in a comparable move to the SG/1 sniping version of the German G3 rifle. Like that design, the Galil is a semi-automatic weapon and also features iron sights as standard.

The sniping version of the Galil fires a 7.62mm round and was developed in close association with the Israeli Defence Forces. The accuracy of the weapon has been

(top) **The Israeli Galil semi-automatic sniping rifle. Note how closely it resembles the standard Galil assault rifle.**

(bottom) **An Israeli soldier carrying a Galil semi-automatic assault rifle.**

determined to be groupings of 120mm to 150mm at a range of 300m, and 300mm at a range of 600m. The standard optical sight for use with the Galil sniping rifle is the Nimrod 6 x 40, which has a sight radius of 475mm. It is mounted on a side bracket fitted to the left-hand side of the weapon, and with this device the accuracy demands are met repeatedly. Whilst the Nimrod is standard to the weapon, the bracket will accept most optical units, including night-vision equipment.

The barrel is longer and heavier than on the standard version of the Galil and has a muzzle brake and flash suppressor to reduce movement and permit the firer to resight quickly after firing. A silencer can be fitted to this weapon, in place of the muzzle brake, to reduce the firing signature, which will allow a sniper to maintain his vantage point for several shots without revealing his position. When firing the weapon with a silencer fitted it is advised that subsonic ammunition be used, as with the Sako TRG.

The Galil sniping rifle can fire either FN match or M118 match ammunition. The standard bipod rest of sniper weapons is fitted behind the fore-end and is fully adjustable to maintain an excellent balance to the weapon and reduce stress to the firer when holding a firing position. The safety catch is located above the pistol grip on the left-hand side of the weapon and the trigger has a two-stage pull. The weapon is fitted with a 20-round box magazine, and has a rotating bolt, but is limited to firing only single rounds for tactical reasons.

The Galil has a folding butt stock, similar to the Swiss SIG 550 sniping rifle, which when locked in place is completely rigid. A fully adjustable cheek-plate is fitted to the butt, and rubber recoil pads can be fitted to the butt-plate to adjust the length of the weapon.

SPECIFICATIONS:

Calibre:	7.62mm x 51
Overall length:	1115mm (butt extended)
	840mm (butt folded)
Weight:	6.4kg (unloaded)
Barrel length:	508mm (excluding muzzle brake)
Rifling:	Four grooves, right hand, one turn in 305mm
Muzzle velocity:	815m/sec with FN match ammunition
	780m/sec with M118 match ammunition

The Russian Army has always made good use of snipers and the effects that long-range sniping has on enemy morale. The current sniping rifle of the Russian Army is the Dragunov SVD which fires the 7.62mm x 54R round. It features many parts common to the standard AK47 rifle, but due to the fact that the Dragunov fires a cartridge 54mm in length as opposed to the more usual cartridge case of 39mm length, the bolt cannot be interchanged.

The operating cycle of the Dragunov, which can be set to single-shot or semi-automatic modes, utilises a short-stroke gas-operated piston. It has a rotating bolt and is fed by a 10-round box magazine. In operation, the piston is forced back on its short stroke by gases which have been tapped off from the barrel during the firing sequence. This imparts force to the bolt carrier which in turn moves back. A lug on the bolt, which moves freely along a special cam path on the carrier, rotates the bolt to unlock it. The bolt and the carrier move together, the return spring is compressed and the carrier moves forward to lock the bolt, thereby allowing firing to take place. Once the carrier has travelled fully home the safety sear is released which frees the hammer for operating by the trigger and the firing pin is struck to fire the round. The trigger mechanism is set for single shots only and this is partly the reason for the simplicity of the design of this weapon.

The Dragunov does not feature a bipod, and the wooden butt stock, which has a cut-out section, is fitted with a removable cheek-plate, but there is apparently no facility to make adjustments to length using butt-plate inserts.

The telescopic sight used with this weapon is the PSO-1 which has a x4 magnification with a six-degree true field of view but a 24-degree apparent field of view. This sight unit is excellent in daytime use and in low light levels is capable of detecting infra-red sources.

Reports claim that the Dragunov is accurate enough to allow target engagement out to ranges of 1,000m, with an effective range estimated to be in the region of 1,300m.

As with other Russian-designed weaponry the Dragunov has been widely copied. There are two copies worth mentioning here, both manufactured by Iraqi State Arsenals: the Al-Kadisa, which is virtually a straight copy of the Dragunov, and the Tabuk, which is similar to the M76 rifle of the former Yugoslavia.

The Al-Kadisa is termed a sniping rifle and fires the same 7.62mm x 54R cartridge as the Dragunov, with which it achieves a muzzle velocity of 830m/sec – identical to the Dragunov's muzzle velocity. The differences between the two weapons appear to be superficial with no obvious modifications. The Al-Kadisa is a semi-automatic rifle using a rotating bolt and is fed by a 10-round box magazine. It weighs 4.3kg, is 1,230 mm in length and has a barrel length of 620mm.

The Tabuk sniping rifle is based on the standard Kalashnikov design and fires the 7.62mm x 39 rimless cartridge. It features a cut-out butt stock and removable cheek-plate similar to the Dragunov, but has a separate pistol grip, whereas the Dragunov and Al-Kadisa both have the pistol grip incorporated into the design of the butt stock. The Tabuk is 1,110mm in overall length, has a barrel length of 600mm and weighs 4.5kg. The effective range of this weapon is understood to be in the order of 600m and it has a muzzle velocity of 740m/sec.

At the height of the Cold War, the Dragunov was issued at the rate of one weapon per platoon in a motor

The Russian Dragunov SVD semi-automatic sniping rifle. Despite its old-fashioned appearance it is still a useful weapon and remains in widespread use in the CIS and former client states of Russia.

rifle unit. Today, there is no reason to believe this rate of issue to be any different.

SPECIFICATIONS:

Calibre:	7.62mm x 54R (Rimmed)
Weight:	4.3kg with PSO-1 sight fitted
Overall length:	1,225mm
Barrel length:	547mm
Rifling:	Four grooves, right hand, one turn in 254mm
Muzzle velocity:	830m/sec

The SG 550 sniping rifle from the Swiss Industrial Company of SIG is one of a mere handful of semi-automatic sniping rifles, and is made even more unusual by the fact that it has a calibre of 5.56mm x 45, which is more usually associated with combat rifles. However, it must be pointed out that some sniping rifles have calibres as low as .22 inch in order to minimise recoil forces and firing signature. These small-calibre rifles are used mainly for engaging targets in urban areas, however, and are unlikely ever to be used on a battlefield.

The SG 550 sniping rifle has been developed from the standard SG 550 assault rifle in co-operation with special units of the police. It is considered to be an appropriate weapon for use in difficult areas, and has even been adopted for use by the Swiss Army. The basic design of this sniping rifle owes much to the SG 550 combat rifle, but there are differences between the two designs which make the sniping version more inherently accurate. The barrel is a heavy hammer-forged design made to precise dimensions and, coupled with the low recoil forces, makes this an easily controlled weapon. The trigger is a sensitive double-pull type, the first

pressure being in the order of 800g and the second being in the order of 1.5kg. This, combined with the gas operation of the weapon, allows the sniper a rapid response, especially if he is required to fire a second shot at the same target.

The weapon is fitted with an ambidextrous safety catch and a bipod which gives good balance to the weapon. The magazine is detachable and has a capacity of either 20 or 30 rounds. For tailoring the weapon to suit individual users, the SG 550 sniping rifle is fitted with fully adjustable cheek-plates and butt stock, which can be folded. The angle of inclination on the pistol grip can also be altered, as can the hand rest.

A gas-operated weapon, the SG 550 has a rotating bolt and fires the Swiss Army's GP90 cartridge, which has high performance and superior precision characteristics that aid accuracy. The SG 550 sniping rifle can be fitted with a wide range of optical sights, including night-vision equipment such as thermal

Exploded diagram showing the components of the Swiss SG 550 version sniper rifle of semi-automatic design.

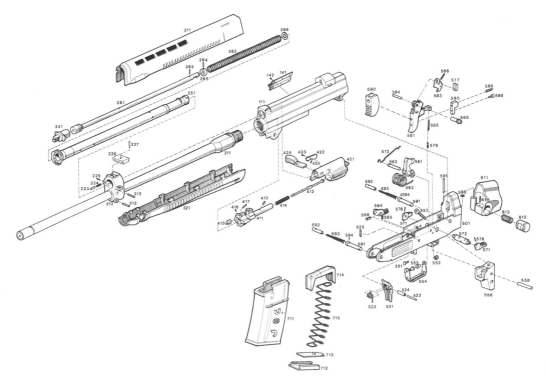

imagers or passive infra-red, to give the sniper a full 24-hour capability. The telescopic sight can be adjusted at right angles to the sight base to give the sniper a more ergonomically designed sighting position. Indeed, the weapon has all the features required to relieve the firer of stress and enable him to remain in a firing position for long periods.

SPECIFICATIONS:

Calibre:	5.56mm x 45
Length:	1,130mm
	905mm with butt folded
Barrel length:	650mm
Length of rifling:	604mm
Rifling:	Six grooves, right hand, one turn in 254mm
Weight:	7.02kg unloaded
Muzzle energy:	Around 1,820J, depending on ammunition

Opposite.

(top) **The SG 550 semi-automatic sniper rifle showing adjustable cheek-plate and butt-plate. The magazine is transparent and the same as used on the infantry's SG 550 assault rifle version.**

(middle) **The SG 550 semi-automatic sniping rifle seen from the left-hand side. Note the adjustable cheek-plate, butt-plate and hand stop on the pistol grip.**

(bottom) **Close-up detail of the bipod and muzzle of the SG 550 semi-automatic sniping rifle.**

Close-up detail of the SG 550 semi-automatic sniping rifle, showing the butt stock in the folded position and the telescopic sight.

Considering the relatively small size of the country, and the fact that it is neutral, Switzerland produces a remarkably comprehensive range of small arms and other weaponry. The SIG-Sauer SSG 2000 sniping rifle is another fine example of this capability and is in widespread use with many police forces, including the Malaysian Police, the Police Force of the Kingdom of Jordan, the Combined Service Forces of Taiwan, some British police forces, and, of course, some Swiss police forces.

The SSG 2000 is a purpose-made sniping weapon available in four calibres including the 7.62mm x 51 cartridge, and is fed from a four-round box magazine. Other calibres in which the SSG 2000 is available are the .300 Weatherby Magnum and the Swiss calibres of 5.56mm x 45 and 7.5mm x 55. It uses a bolt action with hinged lugs mounted at the rear of the bolt which drive outwards to lock into the receiver. This is performed by the action of cams which are driven by the rotation of the bolt handle, the bolt body itself being non-rotating. This latter feature makes for positive case extraction after firing. This might sound like an unusual design feature, but reducing the angular travel of the bolt to some 65 degrees gives a rapid and smooth loading action.

The barrel of the SSG 2000 is manufactured from hammer-forged metal and is fitted with a combination flash suppressor and muzzle brake, which imparts good weapon control and permits the firer to recover his firing position very quickly and compose himself in readiness for a second shot. The trigger mechanism is of the double set type. The standard take-up pull is in the order of 18N, reducing to just 3N when 'set'. The safety catch is a sliding action type which can function in three modes, and can block the sear, the sear pivot and the bolt itself. The bolt can be operated when the safety catch is applied; furthermore the set trigger can be eased by squeezing it when the rifle is in the safe condition, and it is automatically de-cocked when the bolt is opened. To indicate the state of the weapon to the firer there is a signal pin to inform when there is a round in the chamber.

The SSG 2000 rifle can be mounted on a fully adjustable tripod mount to allow moving targets to be tracked. The rifle has a butt stock which incorporates a

vestigial thumb hole and features adjustable cheek-plate and butt-plate spacers to allow for length. The rifle does not feature iron sights in its basic form and will accept a wide range of optical sights, including night-vision equipment. A typical telescopic unit would be either the Schmidt & Bender 1.5-6 x 42 or the Zeiss Diatal ZA 8 x 56T.

SPECIFICATIONS:

Calibre:	7.62mm x 51
Weight:	6.6kg (including scope and loaded)
Overall length:	1,210mm
Barrel length:	610mm (excluding muzzle brake)
Rifling:	Four grooves, right hand, one turn in 305mm
Muzzle velocity:	Typically in the order of 750m/sec depending on ammunition

The Swiss-made SSG 3000 from SIG is a precision-made rifle which, in the hands of a well-trained marksman, will produce consistent results of the highest order. The SSG 3000 is a bolt-action rifle firing the standard NATO 7.62mm x 51 calibre round. The bolt itself has six locking lugs to provide a positive gas seal. The weapon uses the very latest in weapon design technology and has been developed using the Sauer 200 STR target rifle as its base.

The rifle is a modular design with the trigger system and five-round capacity magazine forming a single unit which is fitted into the receiver housing, which in turn is joined to the barrel by screw clamps. The receiver housing is machined from a single block with locking between the bolt and the barrel, which minimises the stress transference to the receiver. The stock of the SSG 3000 is made from non-warping wood laminate to

(top) **View along the right-hand side of the SSG 3000 sniping rifle, showing bipod details, bolt handle and telescopic sight.**

(bottom) **The SSG 3000 sniping rifle shown here in its transportation case with compartments for telescopic sight, spare magazines and bolt.**

(top) **The SSG 3000 sniping rifle seen from the right-hand side, with bipod removed.**

(bottom) **The SSG 3000 sniping rifle seen from the left-hand side showing the adjustable cheek-plate and bipod which is also adjustable.**

(middle) **A police marksman takes aim with the SSG 3000 sniping rifle. He is using the rifle resting on a hard surface and**

has collapsed the bipod legs.

produce a weapon that is low maintenance and simple to use.

The trigger has two take-up weights, which can be adjusted to assist in tailoring the weapon to individual firers. The first take-up weight of the trigger is between 13N and 15N, and the second between 13N and 17N. The safety catch is mounted above the trigger and serves to lock the trigger, bolt and firing pin when applied. The firer can release the safety catch without having to change position, which increases his response time. There is a cocking indicator pin with red and white surfaces at the end of the striker head to indicate to the firer the state of the weapon. The firing pin is light and has only a short distance to travel before striking the base of the round, thereby giving an extremely short lock time.

The heavy barrel of the SSG 3000 is manufactured from cold-swaged metal and has a combined muzzle brake and flash suppressor, which has a significant influence on the accuracy and stability of the weapon. It has a fully adjustable cheek-plate and butt-plate and a bipod, all of which can be fitted to suit the anatomy of individual firers. The SSG 3000 is also available in a left-handed version.

The weapon has no iron sights, due to the fact that it is intended to be used solely with telescopic sights. It can accept most optical sights, including night-vision equipment and NATO STANAG equipment, but the Hensoldt 1.5-6 x 42BL has been specifically designed for use with the SSG 3000. This sight unit is attached to the rifle by means of a mounting which allows for axial adjustment to suit individual users' eye relief length. For training or practice purposes a .22 inch conversion kit is available for this weapon.

SPECIFICATIONS:	
Calibre:	7.62mm x 51 NATO
Length overall:	1,180mm
Weight unloaded:	5.4kg
	6.2kg (with Hensoldt sight fitted)
Length of barrel:	600mm (excluding flash suppressor)
Rifling:	Four grooves, right hand, one turn in 305mm
Feed:	5-round box magazine
Muzzle velocity:	800m to 830m per second, depending on ammunition
Muzzle energy:	3,500 to 3,750 Joules, depending on ammunition

Exploded diagram of the SSG 3000 sniping rifle.

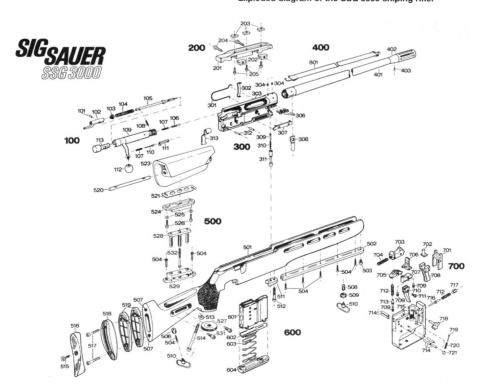

89

Although no longer in service use with the British Army, the L42A1 sniping rifle, or variants of it, are likely to be encountered from time to time. The L42A1 was introduced into service with the British Army in order to meet the requirements for a specialised sniping rifle. It is essentially a No.4 Lee-Enfield converted to fire 7.62mm ammunition instead of the .303 inch round, and as such is a standard bolt-action rifle.

The rifles converted for the sniping role were either No.4 Mark I (T) or No.4 Mark I* (T), which, as mentioned at the start of this chapter, were already used for the role of sniping, and were fitted with the No.32 Mark 3 telescope. The L42A1 differs from other variants by having its trigger pinned to the trigger guard and not mounted on the receiver as on the L39A1 version. The

trigger has a two-stage take-up, with the first pull being set between 1.36kg and 1.81kg and the second set between 2.27kg and 2.95kg.

The detachable box magazine holds ten rounds of 7.62mm NATO, the same number of rounds as the .303 inch version. The firer can also insert single rounds if necessary to 'top up' the magazine. There are subtle differences between the two types converted, but any differences in the results they deliver are marginal. For example, the bolt head on the No.4 Mk.I has a catch on it which must be depressed to allow the bolt-head to either engage or disengage with the guide rib. The No.4 Mk.I*, on the other hand, has a break in the guide rib, but no catch. The mounting brackets for the L1A1 straight sighting telescopic sight are fitted to the left-hand side of the rifle's body, and these also permit image intensifier

The British L42A1 sniping rifle being shown to visiting delegates at a firepower demonstration before it was replaced by the L96A1 rifle.

A British Army sniper leaves the podium after showing the L42A1 sniping rifle to an audience of visiting delegates.

units to be used. The L1A1 telescopic sight is actually a modified No.32 Mk.3 sight of the No.4 (T) rifle. The open sights of the rifle's original design have been retained and the Mk.1 rear sight is used.

To make allowances for the difference in ammunition types, the datum line has been lowered by 1.78mm and the modified slide marked with an 'm' on the right side. The foresight unit is a spit block sweated onto the barrel, with an adjustment screw to allow the sight blade to be clamped to the block. In fact, there are eight sizes of foresight for zeroing, ranging from 0.762 to 1.905mm in increments of 0.381mm. The safety catch on the L42A1 is exactly the same as for the No.4 Lee-Enfield and is located on the left-hand side of the weapon just above the trigger mechanism.

SPECIFICATIONS:

Calibre:	7.62mm x 51mm
Action:	Manual rotating bolt
Weight:	4.43kg
Length overall:	1,181mm
Barrel length:	699mm
Rifling:	Four grooves, right hand, one turn in 305mm
Muzzle velocity:	838m/sec

The AW series of sniper rifles is produced by the same British company, Accuracy International in Hampshire, who also designed the L96A1 sniping rifle as used by the British Army. On first glance the two weapons bear a remarkable likeness, but investigation reveals them to be completely separate systems.

In the AW series there are three versions of the weapon, all of which use detachable magazines of ten-round capacity, except for the 'SM' version which uses a five-round capacity magazine. The AW and AWS, the 'suppressed' version, both fire the NATO 7.62mm x 51 round (.308 Win) and the AWP also fires a 7.62mm round. The SM, 'Super Magnum', version fires a .338 LAP MAG (.300 Win Mag) round.

The range of rifles in this series can accept many different types of telescopic sight, but there are recommended sights for use with a specific weapon,

including night-vision equipment. For example, the AW and AWS are likely to be fitted with a Hensoldt 10 x 42,

(top) **The AW series is the latest design from a British manufacturer of sniping rifles and is based on the earlier, and highly successful, L96A1 design. The Model AWP optimises all that is inherently required of a sniping rifle. It is seen here fitted with a Schmidt and Bender 12x50 variable power scope for excellent target acquisition over all ranges and is currently in service with a large number of military units and law enforcement agencies.**

(bottom) **This is another in the AW series of sniping rifles and is designed to be highly accurate over all ranges, even in low light level conditions, and has a number of reliable safety features. Night vision units can be fitted to permit the weapon to be used in all conditions.**

while the AWP would feature the Schmidt and Bender 3-12V x 50. The type of optical unit fitted to the SM rifle depends on the end user's choice. Each of the designs in this range is fitted with an adjustable bipod, but unlike the Counter Terrorist version of the L96A1, they do not feature a spike in the butt stock.

The AW series of rifles has been designed to permit complete interchangeability of parts, including the barrel and bolt action, with the maintenance of correct head space. The bolt is a three lug design and operates well in adverse conditions such as sub-zero temperatures and heavy fouling, such as sand. In fact, the rifles can be used in conditions with temperatures as low as -40°C. The AWP version has been developed specifically to meet the requirements of Special Forces units and other groups mounting internal security operations. The AW version has been NATO codified and the action can be supplied with either a three or six forward lug bolt system.

Test firings using four weapons have revealed very little wear even after 10,000 rounds. Only the barrel, which is stainless steel throughout the series, showed some wear. The tests were conducted without maintenance being carried out on the weapons and resulted in few, if any, part failures and misfeeds, or other malfunctions.

The AWS 'suppressed' version is basically an AW rifle with an integrated barrel and suppressor interchanged for the normal barrel. This action takes some three minutes to perform and full power ammunition can be used. With the suppressor the AWS can be used out to ranges of 300m, with a signature noise less than the report of a .22LR round.

The 'SM' Super Magnum version is available in 8.60mm x 70 calibre, which usefully closes the gap left between the conventional calibres of 7.62mm and the much larger .50 inch calibre 'anti-material' rifles. The SM is usually supplied with a Bausch and Lomb Tactical 10x telescopic sight, but it can be fitted with whichever sight unit the firer prefers. The inherent accuracy and high power of this rifle extends the effective range for serious anti-personnel sniping by some 35 per cent, to ranges of 1,100m and beyond.

The SM is also available in .300 Win Mag and 7mm Rem Mag, and is interchangeable between calibres by

(top) **The AWS is a fully suppressed version of the AW series of sniping rifle and has been developed to give law enforcement agencies a low signature weapon for use in urban situations. A number of sniping rifles can be fitted with suppressors, but the signature of the AWS is comparable to the report from a .22 inch LR round, which is virtually negligible. Full power ammunition can be used with the AWS without unduly shortening the service life of the suppressor. However, the re-calibration of sights is highly advised.**

(bottom) **This version of the standard AW series sniping rifle is fitted with the Hensoldt 10x42 scope to illustrate the versatility of the weapon's design in being fitted with various types of optical units which increase its usefulness in all situations.**

changing the bolt head, magazine and barrel. The stock is formed from reinforced nylon and is fitted over the entire length of the rifle, with the two halves being held together by Allen screws, in the same manner as the L96A1. The butt stock can be adjusted in length by inserting or removing spacer plates and the pistol grip is formed into part of the butt stock to provide a vestigial thumb hole.

SPECIFICATIONS:

	AW & AWS	AWP	SM
Calibre:	7.62mm x 51	7.62mm x 51	.338 LAP MAG
	(.308 Win)	(.308 Win)	(.300 Win Mag)
Weight:	6.4kg	6.8kg	7.0kg
Length:	1,180mm (AW)	1,100mm	1,200mm
	1,200mm (AWS)		
Barrel:	660mm	610mm	610–686mm

All sniping rifles are transported, where practical, in a specially constructed transportation box. This box is capable of absorbing normal handling during transportation to the site of deployment and contains all the necessary items required for use and maintenance, such as spare magazines, cleaning kit, butt stock spacers for length adjustment and other ancillary items. The box protects the rifle and the delicate telescopic sight unit when being moved over long distances.

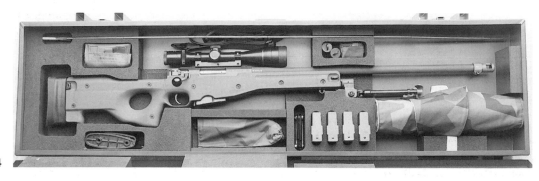

The British Army's latest sniping rifle is termed the L96A1 and fires the 7.62mm x 51 cartridge. It is designed by a British company and was chosen for service over the Parker-Hale M85 rifle following a competitive series of trials and field shoot-offs.

The L96 is designed to be effective, yet have a straightforward operating system without compromising safety. The whole stock furniture of the rifle comprises two halves bolted together, but is so designed as to allow access to component parts for maintenance and cleaning. The trigger assembly is fully adjustable, having a take-up pull of between 1kg and 2kg, and can be removed without the need to dismantle the whole rifle. The entire stock can be stripped away in approximately

five minutes using only a screwdriver and an Allen key.

The barrel is manufactured from stainless steel and is fitted to the body of the rifle by means of a threaded breech end, and is of the type known as 'floating'. This means that it is unsupported along its entire length and is fixed to the body of the rifle only at the breech. This design is well accepted for sniper rifles and does not upset the zeroing of the rifle under normal handling conditions. On the L96A1 barrel changing can be completed in less than five minutes without having to strip the rifle down.

The L96A1 is bolt-action with multi-lug design and uses detachable box magazines with ten-round capacity. The rifle is fitted with a detachable bipod, which is fully adjustable and can be used in conjunction with a retractable spike in the butt stock to form a tripod base for use if the sniper has to maintain his position for prolonged periods. The butt stock is adjustable in length by fitting or removing spacers and the overall configuration has been designed for ambidextrous use.

The L96A1 has iron sights as standard but in the military sniping role is usually fitted with PM 6 x 42 telescopic sights. The 'Counter Terrorist' version of the

(left) **A British Army sniper in his firing position takes aim with the L96A1 sniping rifle.**

(bottom) **A British Army sniper takes position behind a tree for camouflage whilst using the L96A1 sniping rifle.**

rifle, for use by law enforcement agencies, is usually fitted with the PM 21/2-10 x 56 telescopic sight. The rifle is capable of accepting most night-sight units, including the Pilkington 'Kite', and other sighting units such as the KN250 and OE 8050 Individual Weapon sight. The weapon can also be supplied in the 'moderated' or low signature version for use in urban situations.

SPECIFICATIONS:

Calibre.	7.62mm x 61
Weight:	6.50kg
Length:	1,124mm to 1,194mm
Barrel:	655mm

A British Army sniper emerges from his hide holding the L96A1 sniping rifle. He is wearing a Ghillie suit to aid him in concealing himself when firing at the enemy in the combat area.

Close-up detail of the bolt action and telescopic sight of the British Army's L96A1 sniping rifle.

The Parker-Hale M85 sniping rifle was designed by the British company bearing that name with the intention of supplying the British Army. However, it was pipped at the post by the L96A1 in a final shoot-off. According to one source from the British Army's Small Arms School at Warminster, in Wiltshire, there was not a great deal between the two weapons. The weapon is no longer manufactured in the United Kingdom. In 1990 Parker-Hale sold the manufacturing rights to the Gibbs Rifle Company in America, who are still manufacturing the weapon and supplying various end users.

The M85 was designed to give the firer a 100 per cent first-round hit capability out to ranges of 600m. It is fitted with a specially designed action, which has a built-

in aperture rear sight – adjustable for ranges out to 900m – for use in an emergency. The M85 features an integral dovetail mounting to allow a wide variety of telescopic sights and night-vision equipment, such as the Simrad KN250, to be fitted, which will permit combat sniping in all conditions, 24 hours a day. The weapon also features a positive return-to-zero and recoil stop.

The M85 fires the standard 7.62mm x 51 round using a detachable ten-round box magazine, and uses the bolt action typical of most sniping rifles of this type. The trigger mechanism is all steel and has the double pull action set between 0.9kg and 2.25kg. The safety catch is silent in operation and when applied it locks the bolt sear and trigger.

An adjustable bipod is fitted to the fore-end of the rifle and allows the firer to track a moving target. The bipod folds back along the forestock when not in use and has provision for both swivel and cant adjustments of approximately 14 degrees in each direction, without moving the leg positions. The butt stock is fully adjustable in length by means of insert plates, and the cheek-plate, as well as being adjustable, is also ambidextrous. The M85 sniping kit comes with five insert plates supplied in the carrying box, along with other ancillary items, including spare magazines and cleaning kit. The whole stock of the M85 is cast in one piece from fibreglass

(left) **Close-up detail of the bipod fitted to Parker-Hale's M85 sniping rifle.**

(bottom) **The Parker-Hale M85 sniping rifle seen from the right-hand side, showing the bolt action and detachable ten-round box magazine.**

and is available in NATO green, jungle and desert disruptive pattern, an Arctic disruptive pattern and an urban disruptive pattern. This last design uses dark colours and would be ideal for law enforcement agencies who wish to place their snipers, or 'marksmen', in a low-profile location.

The M85 can also be fitted with a suppressor, for which purpose the muzzle is threaded. The suppressor will handle both supersonic and reduced velocity ammunition and all but eliminates muzzle flash and firing signature. To allow a suppressor to be fitted the firer has only to remove the front sight assembly, by means of an Allen key, which is achieved in very little time. Use of a suppressor on the M85 has the added benefit of reducing the recoil energy when fired, which means a sniper does not have to make adjustments to his aiming position if he is required to fire another shot in quick succession.

When the company of Parker-Hale was manu-facturing the M85 it developed the M86 version of the rifle, which fired 7.62mm rounds from a detachable box magazine but with a five-round capacity. This model was fitted with a micro-adjustable aperture rear sight suitable for ranges in excess of 1,000m. The action of the M86 was also drilled and tapped to receive standard Unertl-type bases for mounting a long tube telescopic sight.

SPECIFICATIONS:

Calibre:	7.62mm x 51
Weight:	5.7kg to 6.24kg, depending on telescopic sight fitted, and with magazine
Length:	1,150mm overall
Butt length:	Adjustable from 315mm to 385mm
Barrel:	700mm
Rifling:	Four grooves, right hand, one turn in 305mm

Opposite.

(top) **The Parker-Hale M85 sniping rifle fitted with an SS80 night-vision sight.**

(middle) **The Parker-Hale M85 sniping rifle with urban camouflage stock. Note the well-constructed bolt action and the fully adjustable bipod.**

(bottom) **The Parker-Hale M85 sniping rifle in its carrying case, complete with cleaning kit, spare magazines and sights.**

(below) **The M86 from Parker-Hale was a development of the M85 sniping rifle and could engage targets out to 1,200m range.**

COMBAT SHOTGUNS

Despite the fact that the shotgun has been used by the military at various times, it has never been readily adopted into service use as an infantry weapon. It is instead seen primarily as a weapon used by police and paramilitary forces, mainly for security purposes.

It was US servicemen serving in the trenches of the First World War who first popularised the use of the shotgun as an effective military weapon for use in confined spaces. Known as the 'Trench Gun M1917' the US Army originally bought several thousand short-barrelled riot guns which had been modified to accept bayonets and were fitted with sling swivels. The original cardboard-based cartridges were far too flimsy for conditions in the trenches and brass cases, like rifle cartridges, were soon developed. After the First World War the shotguns were consigned back to the arsenals, re-emerging only when America entered the Second World War following the attack on Pearl Harbor in December 1941. The shotgun was used by US troops in the Pacific theatre of operations, but in Europe it was rarely used by regular troops in combat.

The shotgun in military use is an ideal close-quarter weapon, well suited to use in jungle fighting, house clearing and perimeter security at sensitive military bases. The British Army used shotguns to good effect against the Communist guerrillas during the Malayan campaign in the 1950s. However, it must be pointed out that British troops had to learn from the Malayan police how valuable a shotgun could be in an ambush situation. The British Army at the time purchased several thousand shotguns from the American companies of Browning and Remington. With typical British thoroughness and attention to detail, a report into the effectiveness of shotguns in a combat situation was prepared. With equally British contempt, the report, considered by those who have seen it to be the definitive work of its type on combat shotgun use, was ignored. Even today, this report has only ever been studied by America with any great seriousness.

The use of shotguns by US troops in Vietnam was influenced more by results achieved during the Pacific theatre of the Second World War than anything else. As a result they had to re-evaluate the position of the shotgun in a combat role. The Americans produced their own assessment and it came as no surprise to find that it echoed the British report.

Whilst America is historically seen as the home of the shotgun, relatively little has been done in the US in the way of research into finding means of developing the shotgun into a truly useful combat weapon. Most US military shotguns are simply 'militarised' versions of police models. In Italy, however, the shotgun has been the subject of much research and development, which has concentrated on improving magazine capacity and rate of fire.

Most designs of shotguns used by the military are pump-action, which is to say the slide action has to be pumped in a rearward motion by the firer's forward supporting arm in order to feed and chamber a round from the tubular magazine under the barrel. This means that the number of cartridges held in the tubular

Tear gas grenade, the muzzle attachment for launching and the special propelling cartridge for firing the tear gas grenade. This shows how versatile shotguns can be.

magazine is dictated by the length of the weapon. Conversely, the length of the weapon was determined by the number of cartridges a manufacturer or customer wished to load into the tubular magazine.

The Italian company of Beretta still manufactures a range of conventional shotguns using the slide or pump-action. These weapons have either fixed or folding stocks and are in widespread use with police and paramilitary forces. However, another Italian company, Luigi Franchi, has developed a range of semi-automatic shotguns and even a box magazine-fed weapon, the SPAS 15, which have resulted in the most militarily developed shotguns to date.

Ammunition for shotguns, usually referred to as cartridges, has also been developed way beyond the standard load of lead pellets. A range of non-lethal ammunition has been developed for internal security and riot control use. These include cartridges which discharge a payload of non-penetrating rubber balls, which hurt but lack the kinetic energy of conventional 'rubber bullets'. Another feature for riot control involves a grenade-launching device which is fitted to the muzzle of a shotgun and allows CS gas anti-riot grenades to be fired. More specialised cartridges for police and military roles include 'slug' and 'rifled slug', essentially a heavy ball round capable of penetrating to great depth, and a CS gas-filled cartridge known as 'Ferret' which can be used against fixed or moving targets. The Ferret projectile comprises a plastic carrier which can penetrate glass to deliver its payload of CS gas into a room or a moving vehicle. Other rounds known or believed to be under development for use from a shotgun include a High Explosive Anti-Tank (HEAT) round for engaging lightly armoured vehicles, and flechette for anti-personnel use. These specialised rounds are in addition to the usual cartridges which can be fired from a shotgun. The typical anti-personnel cartridge carries a payload of spherical lead balls approximately 8.4mm in diameter. The terminology is not standardised, and these may be referred to as SG in Britain, or 00 Buck in the United States. The Belgians and Dutch know this size as 9G and the Italians refer to it as 11/0. A 3-inch magnum 12-bore cartridge, containing 1⅝ oz of shot, will fire 13 of these pellets – each one roughly as lethal as a 9mm pistol round.

Today, shotgun cartridges are manufactured from plastic – a material which is lightweight and water-resistant, but stands up well to the rough handling associated with combat situations. The most common shotgun calibre in use with current in-service weapons is referred to as 12-gauge, also known to some users as 12-bore. The gauge or bore size was originally defined by the number of lead balls, fitting exactly in the barrel, which would weigh 1 lb – so a smaller 'gauge' or 'bore' number denotes a larger calibre weapon. A 10-gauge shotgun, for instance, is larger than a 12-gauge.

Range of shotgun cartridges, including slug, non-lethal rubber ball types, conventional pellets and the tear gas 'Ferret' round.

The Beretta RS200 12-gauge shotgun is a conventionally laid out pump-action weapon designed specifically for use by law enforcement agencies. This is a well-made weapon capable of withstanding rough handling under most circumstances. The tubular magazine for the RS200 can accommodate up to six rounds of any nature of 12-gauge ammunition, and with one round ready in the chamber this gives the firer a capacity of seven shots ready for immediate use. The RS200 is fitted with a fixed wooden butt stock, and a special sliding-block locking mechanism prevents accidental discharge before locking is complete. A double bent on the hammer is a further safety precaution to prevent premature discharge of a round and a bolt catch allows the firer to extract a chambered round without firing it.

The RS200 has been declared obsolete but its usefulness and ruggedness mean it is still likely to be encountered. The RS200 can fire all natures of 12-gauge ammunition, including CS gas cartridges, non-lethal rubber balls, ordinary shot and slug.

SPECIFICATIONS:

Calibre:	12-gauge
Operation:	Manual repeating, pump-action
Locking:	Sliding block
Feed:	5 to 6 rounds in tubular magazine
Weight:	3kg
Length Overall:	1,030mm
Barrel length:	520mm
Chamber length:	70mm

This is another Italian-designed shotgun from the manufacturers of the RS200 and is primarily intended for use by law enforcement agencies. In fact, the RS202P is a natural development from the earlier RS200 model and most specifications of that weapon also apply to this one. The main difference between the two designs is the fact that the RS202P has a 'cartridge latch button', which allows the bolt to be operated without releasing the next round from the magazine. This allows the user to load a special purpose round without first emptying the magazine. Furthermore, loading and unloading with the RS202P is easier than on the RS200 shotgun.

There are various designs which make up a range of models available in the basic RS202P pump-action shotgun, each with the capability of being fitted with interchangeable chokes to alter the pattern of shot. One variation is a folding stock version which allows ease of handling in the interior of a vehicle. The model RS202PM3 features a folding stock and barrel cover with rifle sights and an attachment for fitting a telescopic sight and a muzzle diffuser. A telescopic sight is, in fact, rarely fitted to a shotgun. It can make for greater accuracy with rifled slug cartridges, but even then accuracy with these types of cartridge never matches that of a rifle. However, the telescopic sight fitting will also permit other types of sight to be used, including night-vision types.

(top) **The Beretta RS202P shotgun showing its rugged design.**

(middle) **The Beretta RS202P shotgun showing details of the trigger, ejector port for spent cases and the loading 'gate' on the underside just in front of the trigger guard.**

(bottom) **The Beretta RS202P shotgun with folding butt stock.**

(top) **Top: The Beretta RS202P with folding butt stock extended. Bottom: The Beretta RS202PM3 with folding butt stock, barrel cover and special sights and diffuser.**

(middle) **The Beretta RS202P with interchangeable chokes and folding butt stock.**

(bottom) **The Beretta RS202P with folding butt stock in extended position.**

The PA3 range of shotguns was designed and developed by the Italian company of Luigi Franchi and these weapons represent very compact designs of shotguns. The PA3 range comprises the 215 and 345, which have three- and five- round magazine capacity respectively, with an extra cartridge ready in the chamber. Both designs are manufactured from high strength alloy with double operating rods which are made from all machined drawn alloyed steel. Apart from the usual safety catch, which is located on the right-hand side of the trigger plate, the weapon will not function until the breech block is completely locked, and the breech mechanism can only be operated after the hammer has been released.

Both designs are fitted with pistol grips for the firing hand, and the safety catch can be operated without having to remove the hand from the firing position, which makes for a rapid response. The PA3/215 version is a no-frills design, lacking butt stock and sights, which gives it an appearance not dissimilar to the Ithaca 'Stakeout' Model 37. However, unlike that weapon the PA3/215

has a forward pistol grip to assist with the pump-action to eject spent cartridges and rechamber a new round. It has an overall length of only 470mm which makes it an ideal weapon for close quarter protection and possible use by special forces units to remove hinges from doors during rapid entrance operations.

The PA3/345 is a more conventional pump-action shotgun design with a five-round capacity and folding butt stock. This weapon has basic sights and its robust design lends it to being used by either police or paramilitary forces for a wide range of uses, including road blocks, perimeter security and dynamic entry techniques by counter-terrorist forces.

The PA3 range. Top: PA3/215 with forward pistol grip. Bottom: PA3/345 with folding butt stock and standard pump action.

SPECIFICATIONS:

	PA3/215	PA3/345
Calibre:	12-gauge	12-gauge
Magazine capacity:	3 + 1	5 + 1
Barrel length:	215mm	345mm
Overall length:	470mm	840mm
Width	46mm	46mm
Weight unloaded:	2.3kg	2.8kg

Despite the modern appearance of the two designs in this range of shotguns, the models PA7 and PA8 are actually well-established weapons from the Italian company of Luigi Franchi, who also designed the PA3 series and the SPAS 12 and SPAS 15. The main difference between the PA7 and PA8 designs lies in the fact that the former design lacks a pistol grip, giving it a rifle like appearance.

The PA8 shotgun is available in either the 'E' series or 'I' series, which have a fixed or folding butt stock respectively. The weapons in the series can be fitted with either a 475mm or 610mm Magnum Variomix barrel, with a two-round magazine extension also available. The basic weapons already have a five-round tubular magazine capacity, with one in the chamber, and so the ability to have up to eight rounds ready to fire makes this range of shotguns one of the most powerful in service.

All three weapons in this range are conventional pump-action types, and are well-constructed to withstand punishing treatment. Each of the weapons is fitted with rifle sights and features a double safety device within the trigger group as found on the SPAS 12 shotgun.

Variomix chokes, with a barrel extension from 50mm to 150mm, can also be fitted to all three weapons to alter the pattern of the shot.

This range of shotguns can fire all natures of 12-gauge ammunition, including slug. However, when using slug the Variomix choke cannot be fitted. The PA7 and PA8 shotguns are high-profile weapons and are well-suited to the roles of perimeter security and road blocks. In this last role, the weapons could be used to fire CS gas cartridges to penetrate the windscreen to incapacitate, in a non-lethal manner, those drivers who are reluctant to stop.

Top: PA7 with fixed butt stock.

Centre: PA8E with fixed butt stock and pistol grip.

Bottom: PA8I with folding butt stock and pistol grip.

The Italian company of Luigi Franchi has a reputation for producing high-quality shotguns for police and paramilitary use, but when they unveiled their design for the SPAS 12 the company took the shotgun fraternity by storm.

Despite its bulky appearance, the SPAS 12, or Special Purpose Automatic Shotgun, still fires only the standard 12-gauge cartridge of 70mm in length. The tubular magazine capacity can be either six or seven rounds, plus one in the chamber, and the weapon can fire all natures of shotgun ammunition, including slug, non-lethal and anti-vehicle rounds. This is a high-profile weapon of sturdy construction, making it an excellent all-round weapon for both offensive and defensive purposes. It can be supplied with either a folding or fixed butt stock, depending on the operational role.

The SPAS 12 has the normal functions of standard pump-action type shotguns, but it can be switched to gas operated semi-automatic fire simply by depressing a button on the forestock. This feature is particularly useful in allowing the firer rapidly to fire heavy loads to suppress a target, although at the cost of the weapon being difficult to control.

The very nature of the SPAS 12's appearance makes it a psychological deterrent in most situations. Indeed, it has often been considered by special forces, due to its versatility and high rate of fire. A practical rate of fire with the SPAS 12 is considered to be in the region

The Italian SPAS 12 shotgun.

(top) **Overall view of weapon with folding stock.**

(bottom) **Close-up detail of the barrel and forestock.**

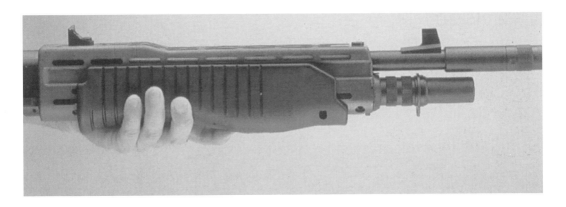

of 24 to 30 rounds per minute, but in the semi-automatic mode it is capable of 250 cyclic rounds per minute.

The SPAS 12 has front and rear sights fitted, and the bodywork is manufactured from a special anti-shock resin.

The SPAS 12 is a purpose-built shotgun, not one which has been militarised from a design which started life as a sporting weapon. The author has experience in firing this weapon, and whilst it is quite a 'fistful', after a few rounds it felt comfortable once the firing sequence had been accepted as being so much different from ordinary pump-action shotguns.

Safety features on the SPAS 12 include the normal safety catch by the trigger mechanism, plus there is also a lock-up safety with plunger in order to block the hammer, and a safety on the trigger lever to make it doubly safe when operating from a vehicle.

SPECIFICATIONS:

Calibre:	12-gauge x 70mm
Type:	Pump-action slide and semi-automatic gas-operated (selectable)
Feed:	6-7; plus one in chamber
Barrel length:	460mm or 550mm
Overall length:	710mm (460mm barrel and stock folded)
	930mm (460mm barrel and stock extended)
Weight:	4.1kg

Following on the success of its SPAS 12 design, the Italian company of Luigi Franchi once more turned its attention to perfecting a shotgun which was more in keeping with military requirements. The result was the SPAS 15, or Special Purpose Automatic Shotgun 15, which is as far removed from tubular magazine shotguns as these are in turn from double-barrel shotguns.

With the SPAS 15, the company of Franchi has overcome the problem of how pump-action shotguns could be quickly reloaded, which was one of the stumbling blocks with other designs. Franchi simply looked at alternative methods and came back to the reliable box magazine method which is fed from underneath, in the same manner as a conventional rifle. Indeed, the SPAS 15 has the appearance of a bulky rifle, with its integral top-mounted carrying handle and box magazine in place.

The SPAS 15 can be operated by the usual pump-action method but, like its predecessor, the SPAS 12, it can be converted to gas-operated semi-automatic fire simply by engaging a conversion button located on top of the forestock. In this mode, the SPAS 15 taps gas from the barrel and feeds it into the gas chamber mounted above the barrel to operate the working parts in the same way as an assault rifle functions. The bolt is a rotating-head design to give the best and most reliable feeding and ejection action possible.

The SPAS 15 is available with either a fixed or folding stock and can fire all natures of 12-gauge ammunition,

including smoke, CS gas, non-lethal rubber ball, slug, steel anti-vehicle piercing, and standard buckshot. The weapon can also be fitted with discharger cups to allow smoke and CS gas grenades to be launched into buildings or to project them to longer ranges than possible with hand-thrown projectiles.

The SPAS 15 is a dual-purpose weapon, being well-suited to both offensive and defensive roles. It can be fitted with a laser-designating device mounted on the top carrying handle to identify positively selected targets. It is marginally lighter in weight than the SPAS 12 and its dimensions are comparable to that weapon. However, the practicalities of it being magazine-fed, and therefore easier to reload, make it a more viable military choice than most other shotguns. There are other magazine-fed shotguns available, but the SPAS 15 has the appearance and rugged endurance required of a real combat shotgun.

The weapon has a double safety feature, the first being the normal safety catch by the trigger guard, which is positively operated. The second safety feature is fitted into the pistol grip and is released by the gripping action of the firing hand. The magazine, which has a capacity

The advanced design of the Italian SPAS 15 with box magazine feed. It has a folding butt stock and is an ideal weapon for use in house-clearing operations.

111

of six rounds, is loaded into the weapon from underneath, as on a rifle, and the cocking handle is located on the upper surface of the receiver under the carrying handle, in a manner similar to the French FAMAS rifle.

The magazine release catch is located behind the magazine and just in front of the trigger guard, which makes for speedy reloading in combat situations. Magazines can be colour-coded, so that the firer can instantly identify the nature of the ammunition in each magazine and can load his weapon according to the situation. The rigid stock is manufactured from anti-shock resin material and the folding stock is manufactured from pressed alloys.

SPECIFICATIONS:

Calibre:	12-gauge x 70mm
Type:	Pump-action slide and semi-automatic gas-operated (selectable)
Feed:	6-round box magazine, plus one round in the chamber
Barrel length:	406mm
Overall length:	1,000mm with fixed stock
	980mm with folding stock extended
	700mm with folding stock folded
Width:	49mm
Weight:	3.90kg (unloaded)
Weight of empty magazine:	0.45kg

The security forces in South Africa have a long history of using shotguns to break up and disperse rioters. The types of shotguns used in these situations tend to be conventionally laid out weapons, but local arms manufacturers have invested time and effort to produce some very forward-thinking firearms.

In the early 1980s the 12-gauge 'Striker' made an appearance, and its design left no-one in any doubt that it was intended for use as an offensive weapon during operations involving street fighting or house clearing. The Striker utilised a spring-wound 12-shot rotary magazine which could be pre-loaded to allow the firer to use various natures of ammunition. The Striker was cylinder-bored to permit the firing of either shot or slug cartridges. Some 13 years after Striker was intended to enter production, the author saw at a major defence exhibition a weapon on a South African defence manufacturer's stand with startling similarities to the Striker. It emerged that the weapon in question was called the 'Protecta' and was indeed based on the layout of the Striker.

Whilst the Striker had good potential and hitting power, the Protecta was seen as its natural successor, with improved safety features. The Protecta has a 12-shot revolver action which eliminates the need to wind the driving spring to impart the rotary action required to align the cylinder with the breech. The underlying safety feature of the Protecta is the fact that it cannot be fired unless the double-action trigger is fully depressed in a positive action. This feature, along with the drop-safe hammer-lock, prevents accidental discharge through trigger snagging if the safety catch is disengaged in readiness for use.

It is claimed that the Protecta can be fired single-handed from the hip, but this would produce poorly aimed shots. The weapon has a metal skeleton butt stock which folds up and over along the top of the weapon, and a forward pistol grip. With the butt stock extended the user can fire the weapon from the shoulder in a more controlled manner. With the special Occluded Eye Gunsight (OEG) sight, which is used with both eyes open, the firer can track and engage a moving target, from a man-sized target to a motor vehicle.

The barrel length of the Protecta is only 300mm,

(right) **Close-up detail of the Occluded Eye Gunsight as fitted to the South African Protecta.**

(below) **Overall view of the South African Protecta, showing its two pistol grips, folding butt stock and rotary drum magazine.**

but the manufacturers claim the pattern of shot to be comparable to weapons with barrel lengths twice this size. The Protecta fires standard 12-gauge shotgun cartridges, including non-lethal types such as the 'Thundershot' which produces a loud report and flash, the Baton Single and the Baton Double which discharge one and two rubber balls respectively and are for use in anti-riot situations.

Spent cartridges are automatically ejected from the cylinder which allows the firer to load single rounds to replenish the ammunition capacity as required, with the nature of ammunition appropriate to the situation.

The 'Roadblocker' MAG-10 shotgun from Ithaca has been designed for law enforcement agencies with the sole purpose of providing a force-multiplier to deal effectively with criminals in vehicles. The Roadblocker is unusual in that it is of 10-gauge, which gives it considerably greater power than the standard 12-gauge shotgun cartridge. The cartridge for the Roadblocker is 3.5 inches in length and the tubular magazine holds only three rounds, with a round in the chamber, to give a capacity of four rounds ready to use.

The weapon is gas-operated and considerably heavier than its Model 37 counterparts. The force of the recoil with such a weapon might be considered excessive, but Ithaca has overcome this problem by developing a recoil compensator known as 'Countercoil'. This acts by extending the period during which the recoil force is maintained, reducing it to more controllable levels.

In military terms the Roadblocker has limited usefulness, due largely to its heavy weight and limited ammunition capacity, and is therefore more likely to be used by mobile police and paramilitary forces.

SPECIFICATIONS:

Calibre:	10-gauge x 3.5 inch
Type:	Gas-operated semi-automatic
Feed:	3 rounds in tubular magazine, plus 1 in chamber
Barrel length:	558mm
Weight:	4.87kg

The Ithaca MAG-10 'Roadblocker' showing its heavy construction.

Of all the American-designed shotguns the Ithaca range of Model 37 shotguns is perhaps the most comprehensive. They all follow the straight-line layout of the conventional shotgun design, but the variations in calibre (gauge) and stocks are what make them different.

The Model 37 M&P is available with either a five-shot or eight-shot capacity tubular magazine, with an extra cartridge in the chamber in each case. This version is a 'no-frills' shotgun and is built to withstand punishing treatment. The Model 37 M&P is chambered to accept all natures of standard 12-gauge cartridges of 2.75 inch length. The 'DS' version in the Model 37 range is also available in five- and eight-shot versions, with the standard 'one in the chamber' to increase the

ammunition capacity to six and nine rounds respectively. The 'DS' stands for 'Deerslayer', indicating that this started as a sporting version of the company's range of hunting shotguns. The progression of such a highly

(top) **The Ithaca Model 37 'Deerslayer' Police Special with eight-shot magazine.**

(middle upper) **The Ithaca Model 37 'Deerslayer' Police Special with five-shot magazine.**

(middle lower) **The Ithaca Model 37 Special Los Angeles Police Department Model.**

(bottom) **The Ithaca Model 37 M&P five-shot.**

(top) **The Ithaca Model 37 M&P 8-shot.**

(bottom) **The Ithaca Model 37 'Stakeout' 20 gauge.**

reliable and well-made weapon from sporting roles to law enforcement and military use was a natural evolution.

The action and specifications of the 'DS' are the same as for the basic Model 37 M&P, with the only difference being that the 'DS' is fitted with rifle-type sights. The 'Special LAPD' version of the Model 37 has been developed specifically for use by the Los Angeles Police Department and is available in the five-round version. It features sling swivels for a carrying strap, a recoil pad on the butt stock, fire-interruptor and a special drive-in rear-block sight.

The Ithaca Model 37 'Stakeout' version of the standard Model 37 is a very compact design, lacking a butt stock entirely, and is available in either 20-gauge or 12-gauge calibres. Of these two sizes the 12-gauge is the preferred calibre, with the 20-gauge calibre being developed for personal protection services and intended for use at close quarters. Such roles would include the movement of important personnel from vehicles to buildings by law enforcement agents. Its compact design makes it an ideal weapon for carrying in a concealed manner or for deploying from a light motor vehicle, yet still having a capacity of five rounds in the tubular magazine and an extra round in the chamber.

SPECIFICATIONS:

	Calibre	Action	Capacity	Barrel	Weight
Model 37 M&P	12-gauge	Pump-action	5 or 8 + 1	470mm (5-shot)	2.94kg (5-shot)
and Model 37 'DS'			508mm (8-shot)	3.06kg (8-shot)	
Special LAPD	12-gauge	Pump-action	5 + 1	470mm	2.95kg
Stakeout 12	12-gauge	Pump-action	5 + 1	336mm	2.26kg
Stakeout 20	20-gauge	Pump-action	5-round	336mm	1.58kg